Alaskan Sunrise
to African Sunset

Alaskan Sunrise to African Sunset

Hunting Adventures in the Great Outdoors

Glenn T. Bingham

iUniverse, Inc.
New York Bloomington Shanghai

Alaskan Sunrise to African Sunset
Hunting Adventures in the Great Outdoors

Copyright © 2008 by Glenn T. Bingham

All rights reserved. No part of this book may be used or reproduced by any means, graphic, electronic, or mechanical, including photocopying, recording, taping or by any information storage retrieval system without the written permission of the publisher except in the case of brief quotations embodied in critical articles and reviews.

iUniverse books may be ordered through booksellers or by contacting:

iUniverse
1663 Liberty Drive
Bloomington, IN 47403
www.iuniverse.com
1-800-Authors (1-800-288-4677)

Because of the dynamic nature of the Internet, any Web addresses or links contained in this book may have changed since publication and may no longer be valid.

The views expressed in this work are solely those of the author and do not necessarily reflect the views of the publisher, and the publisher hereby disclaims any responsibility for them.

ISBN: 978-0-595-49375-3 (pbk)
ISBN: 978-0-595-49591-7 (cloth)
ISBN: 978-0-595-61075-4 (ebk)

Printed in the United States of America

This book is dedicated to the memories of my hunting buddies Jim Reape and Steve (Spence) Strife.

Contents

Introduction ix
Chapter 1   An Outdoor Foundation 1
Chapter 2   Dr. Peebles I Presume 4
Chapter 3   Grouse Hunting 101 9
Chapter 4   First Deer 13
Chapter 5   Bow Hunting is Easy 17
Chapter 6   Saskatchewan Silver Tip 22
Chapter 7   Broken Leg Buck 29
Chapter 8   Solo in Montana 34
Chapter 9   Frozen in Saranac 39
Chapter 10   Oxygen, it's a Good Thing 43
Chapter 11   Frozen Hands Buck 47
Chapter 12   Alaskan Adventure 52
Chapter 13   Newfoundland Aye Bye 60
Chapter 14   Mule Deer Education 65
Chapter 15   Heavy Cover Whitetails 74
Chapter 16   Wyoming Double 79
Chapter 17   Way Out There 83
Chapter 18   Flatland Elk, Believe It Or Not 91

Chapter 19	South Africa Adventure	95
Chapter 20	Colorado Dream'n?	109
Chapter 21	When Porcupines Attack	113
Chapter 22	Fog, Wind and Trophy Dalls	117
Chapter 23	Inyati on the Run	125
Chapter 24	More Running in Zimbabwe	134
Chapter 25	Leopard Charge	144
Chapter 26	Golden Gate Elk in the High Country	148
Chapter 27	Canadian Drops and Kickers	155
Chapter 28	A Guide's Life	161
Chapter 29	Nebraska Ducks and Bucks	168
Conclusion		173
Appendix		175

Introduction

I have been lucky enough to spend a great deal of time in the wilderness. I started out as a youngster in upstate New York, and gradually expanded my experiences throughout North America and beyond, culminating with journeys to Alaska and Africa. Each experience fills my mind with memories of adventure. To me the grandeur and sense of adventure when you're out in the boondocks is unparalleled. Nature is not good or bad, it simply exists and you take out of it what you will. Most people on the planet tend to think of themselves as being above or outside of the natural world. I like to think that I'm a part of nature. Sometimes I even get myself into situations where I feel a little lower on the food chain than is comfortable, but that only makes the experience more appealing.

I've been so cold that I had to force my fingers around the butt of my shotgun, because the wood ducks were dumping into the decoys. I've sat on stand waiting for that monster buck, while the snow piled eight inches high on my lap. I've been battered by winds that I could barely stand up against, leaning at an angle that made me look like I was jumping off a ski jump. I've been so hot that it felt like my brain was cooking. I've been on mountain slopes where a slip means death.

I make it sound pretty darned uncomfortable, don't I? But that comes with the territory, and I would not trade it for anything, because I've also stood on mountaintops that haven't felt another human being's steps, watched sunrises and sunsets no one else could see, and breathed the cleanest air on the planet. The uncomfortable times make the successes that much sweeter and the adventure all the more spectacular.

I feel more comfortable out in the bush than anywhere else. There's nothing like being dropped off in the middle of nowhere and watching a plane fly off into the horizon with no way to contact another human being on the planet. I relish those moments, where self-reliance kicks in and the modern world fades. I like being somewhere where the days run together and you don't know whether it's Monday or Wednesday, and it doesn't really matter.

Along the way, there are bits of humor, and the companionship of like minded folks who are dense enough do things like getting up at three thirty in the morning to go sit in the rain waiting for a turkey you could buy in the supermarket for a dollar a pound. I like to live by the axiom that you're only young once, but you can be immature forever. Activities like sitting in a tree for twelve hours straight at twenty below zero sounds unbelievably stupid to the average person. Come to think of it, it might sound stupid to many of the hunters out there too. For me however it's all part of the challenge.

Besides, as the human brain slowly freezes, you can conjure up things to do with duct tape you never even considered before. Where else could you dedicate half a day to figuring out things like why an orange is called an orange, but an apple isn't called a red?

What follows are some of the adventures, trials, tribulations and lessons learned the outdoors has brought to me over the last thirty years or so. Allow me to share some of my world, and impart at least a small bit of the enjoyment it has brought me.

The book was written more or less in chronological order. But because I can barely spell the word I feel no responsibility to adhere rigidly to its limitations. In order to provide the reader with a point of reference, the first chapter presents my introduction to the outdoors. In the second chapter I introduce Dr. John Peebles, a long time friend that I've known since we were kids. He was a major influence in my early years of wanderings through the boondocks. I do ramble fairly close to the present in the chapter, but it's strictly for the entertainment value. I spent most of my teenage years chasing grouse around, so the next chapter is dedicated to the frustrating little balls of fluff, followed directly by the story of taking my first deer. I've enjoyed many years of bow hunting, so chapter five describes my frustrating introduction into the sport as well as a story of a buck taken one Halloween which is simply a gratuitous way to get my nieces picture in the book. Following that, the chapters cover hunting adventures in Saskatchewan, Alberta, Montana, New York, Utah, Alaska, Newfoundland, Colorado, Wyoming, Nebraska, South Africa, and Zimbabwe. The game pursued (not necessarily taken) include grouse, turkeys, whitetails, mule deer, pronghorn antelope, caribou, Dall sheep, elk, moose, African plains game, and cape buffalo. There are a few detours along the way, with chapter seventeen describing my journey from a marginal marksman to something slightly better than a marginal marksman along with a few helpful tips that have worked for me. Another detour is chapter twenty one with a few of the more amusing experiences I've had in the outdoors. So pour yourself your favorite beverage, sit back, and enjoy a few adventures in the great outdoors.

Chapter 1
An Outdoor Foundation
1970's–Early 1980's

My paternal grandfather was quite a pheasant hunter in central New York back when there were serious numbers of birds present. My great grandfather actually held several patents for various fishing items. My father also did some fishing and small game hunting growing up. Somewhere along the line his priorities were horribly disrupted and he stopped hunting. I can barely even think about it. He continued fishing, so he didn't have a total breakdown with his values. In fact, my parents used to tie me to a tree while they were fishing, so they wouldn't have to use the net on me as I floated by.

About the time I was eight or nine a friend of my fathers invited him on a ruffed grouse hunt. He went a few times and didn't get anything. One day, he came home with a grouse that his friend had shot. That pretty much did it for me, I had to get into the action. I tagged along from then on.

When I turned ten my parents built a house out in the country with instant access to the wilderness out the front door or the back door. In the mid 1970's there weren't many deer in upstate New York, so much of the land was not posted and was open to the public. Grouse numbers were also at an unbelievable peak. One day, on the neighbor's land across the street, over forty grouse were flushed without the use of a dog. Unfortunately I was still too young to have gun in my hand, but I enjoyed the experience nonetheless. Around this time, my father also started to duck hunt and I spent many hours in a blind watching ducks dumping into the decoys. One day my grandfather was up for a visit and we went out back grouse hunting. He had never hunted grouse before and had not been pheasant hunting for several years. He was shooting an old full choke pump shotgun that had the bluing worn in that neat way that indicates a lot of use, not abuse. With the first bird that flushed under his feet he successfully resisted the urge to yell "Hen!" and shot well behind the bird. He turned to my father and said, "I guess I've got to be a little quicker on these things." With the next bird that flushed, the gun came smoothly to his shoulder and the grouse dropped in a puff of feathers. A simple "Yup," was all he said as he walked over to pick up the bird.

Members of the family raised grapes in the Finger Lakes of central New York, and my uncle, Tom Mitchell was one of them. He was quite a bird and deer hunter, and got my father involved in deer hunting. Of course I ended up tagging along, and loved the experience. This all set the stage for a life in the outdoors.

When I was finally old enough to hunt, Marvin Tyler, a friend of my fathers loaned me a single shot twenty gauge. I don't recall the gun's make, but it was one of those guns that you had to pull back the hammer with your thumb in order to shoot. I don't recall if it actually had a safety, but I never left it in the cocked position, always waiting for a bird to flush before cocking it. This made me very slow on the draw, but I made up for it by being a bad shot.

Once I was old enough to hit the woods by myself I graduated to a JC Higgins twelve gauge full choke that my grandfather had. It wasn't unusual for me to strap the snowshoes on in the morning and head out into the bush. I'd walk for hours and then return in the afternoon. It was always amusing to come back on the same trail I walked out on and find my stride to be too short to step in the same tracks. That's a good kind of being tired. After experimentation, I had specific routes that I'd walk on various pieces of property, normally designed to push the birds out of the unbelievably thick cover into the believably thick cover. Sometimes it worked, sometimes it didn't, but I enjoyed it all anyway.

There was one Christmas where my grandparents asked me what I wanted and I said, "Shotgun shells." Yup, that's all I wanted, and I burned up a bunch of them. Over time and a lot of gunpowder I actually got to be a pretty good shot with the old JC Higgins. In the fall of 1979, the bird numbers were up pretty good and I ended up taking thirty-nine birds without a dog, averaging a bird every two shots in the thick stuff. I'd probably be lucky to average a bird a box right now. My crowning achievement as a grouse hunter was one day when I went out in the morning and took two grouse with two shells, then went out with my father in the afternoon and taking two more with two shells. Of course the next day I think I missed five straight. I hate averages....

From left to right: Author, Bob Shew, Stan Bingham, Mike Shew, Doug Nichols and Paul Nichols following a duck hunt in 1975. Hunts like this kindled the author's passion for the outdoors.

One summer I went to work for my aunt and uncle, Tom and Marcelle Mitchell, cutting suckers off the vines and pulling weeds in their vineyards located in the Finger Lakes of central New York. I quickly found that the foliage was so thick that it didn't let any breeze blow through at all, and during the middle of the day it got extremely hot. I finally changed my hours so I'd drive to the vineyard just as it started to get light, work till eleven or so, and then return in the evening for a few hours. Why did I put myself through this? A nice shiny new semi automatic Remington 1100 with a modified choke was sitting in a store with my name on it. My father had bought one a year or so earlier, and I wanted one desperately. Shortly after my return home, I was walking into the house with a green box and a smile on my face. I quickly found that the best thing about the gun was the amount of ammunition you could put through it in a very short period of time.

The foundation had been laid. The world of the outdoors awaited, with each experience fueling a desire for more.

Chapter 2
Dr. Peebles I Presume
1967–Present

The sun beat down on us mercilessly and we slowly crawled through the foot high grass. It offered very little cover, but it was our only chance to get close and make the shot. I don't know how long we'd been crawling, but it seemed like forever as the sweat rolled off my brow into my eyes. He popped his head up from feeding and we froze. I glanced over at John and he looked about like I felt. We conferred briefly and decided that we were close enough to take the shot. Using a technique we had perfected years before to make sure we anchored dangerous game, we got into shooting position, and I whispered one, two, three. On the silent four, two rifle shots sounded as one and he dropped in his tracks.

Were we in Tanzania hunting cape buffalo? Nope, we were teenagers hunting woodchucks in the fields out behind John's house with twenty two's. While he recently stopped talking to me because I admitted that not only did I know what the word "mulch" meant, I had actually used some around my house, I've been friends with Dr. John Peebles for almost forty years. That makes him really old. I first met John when we were about five years old. He didn't go by Dr. Peebles back then, obviously so he wouldn't intimidate the other kids in class. It was apparent even at that young age that we were kindred spirits with the same warped sense of humor.

Much of my misspent youth in the wilderness was spent with John. Normally cold, wet or muddy, and frequently, bloody. We started hunting as soon as the law would allow. There were no deer to speak of, so we concentrated on pigeons, grouse, woodchucks and the occasional duck or goose. There was generally more shooting than getting, but it was always a good time. Before we got motorized transportation, if we couldn't con a ride out of someone we'd walk to each other's houses, which was about two miles by road or a mile and a half through the swamp. I remember walking along the road that led into town before sunrise with a rifle or shotgun on my shoulder and thinking nothing of it. Imagine what people would think today if they saw a teenager with a gun during the hours of darkness.

We grew up in ideal locations, both of us being out in the boondocks. There was only one channel on TV so hunting and fishing took up most of our free time. John had a set of railroad tracks in back of his place for instant access to a lot of land, and I had woods out the front and back doors of my house. I learned early on that if I was hunting with John, I should bring rain gear. A clear sunny day could produce a gully washing deluge inside of three minutes from the time John stepped out of the house.

Our adventures really picked up when my great Uncle Paul Field gave me his '67 Buick Special. It was fairly rusted out, and had just short of a million miles on it, but to me it was the greatest machine in the world. Out of necessity, my parents were experts in bondo and sheet metal work, so the car underwent some extensive surgery and a paint job. That Buick took me all the way through college and to my first job.

Once we discovered bow hunting, bow fishing and spearing carp during the spring became one of our favorite past times. The only drawback about this endeavor was that spearing carp from a canoe was not the most stable platform in the world. We were floating along placidly one sunny spring day in one of the bays off Lake Ontario. I turned around to say something to John just in time to see him perform a near perfect barrel role over the side of the canoe. While I was contemplating what kind of score I would give the performance, he immediately levitated out of the water, spitting swamp goo and saying something about hypothermia. I started laughing so hard I thought I was going to break a rib. Shortly after that I turned around again and I was dumped into the drink myself. John said the only thing he saw were my feet disappearing over the gunwale. I believed my entrance into the water produced much less of a splash than John's, and the level of difficulty was slightly higher, thereby making it a much better fall. John disagreed, and we discussed the merits of each fall as we tried to dry out. I don't know why I bothered since I ended up right back in the water shortly after that, and then once more before the end of the day.

John was along on one of the best days of smallmouth fishing I've seen, on a very nasty day. My father pulled the boat out of the launch and into Hardscrabble Bay on Lake Ontario. A solid west wind piled the waves into the bay, running four to six feet high and the sky boiled with steel gray clouds. We slowly made our way up to the mouth of the bay and started our first drift. I climbed onto the deck of the sixteen foot Starcraft to allow John and dad a little extra room and started fishing. We started hitting the fish right away, and each drift was producing. One drift in particular stands out. I happened to be looking out toward the stern of the boat when John said he had one on. At that very instant, the biggest bass I'd ever seen cleared the water by two feet. I made some exclamation and scurried back into the boat and grabbed the net. I told dad that John had a monster on, and gave John all the support I could by telling him that he'd go overboard if he lost the fish.

After an epic wrestling match John finally brought the fish to net, and we pulled him into the boat. After congratulations, we measured the fish at twenty and a half inches. We didn't have a scale, but the fish was a monster. We normally ended up with one or two nineteen inch smallmouths each season, but surpassing twenty inches was very rare. We continued to fish and shortly had our limit of bass with several big perch thrown in for good measure. It was a great day of fishing, even with the wind pounding us.

As the time has flown by, I still get a chance to hunt and fish with John occasionally, but jobs and responsibilities have put a damper on our fun. Speaking of responsibilities, after not learning his lesson with wife number one, John decided that he needed a wife number two (or as some people call her, "Karen"). Karen also had not learned her lesson with husband number one and decided that John should be husband number two. They were a perfect match, with both of them apparently having the same learning disability. Karen insisted on bringing her kids along on the deal and John became an instant father. Aaron and Ashley were good kids, though it's not appropriate to ever repeat that.

Shortly after the marriage, or collision, or what ever it's called, I invited John and Aaron down to my camp in the Finger Lakes for some turkey hunting. I'd say Aaron was around ten or eleven years old at the time. I was using diaphragm calls and Aaron decided that he wanted to try one. I grabbed one out of my pack, instructed him on how it was used and sat back to watch the show. At the very first hint of vibration from the call against his tongue he made a face like he had just swallowed a bucket full of lemons and he grabbed the call out of his mouth like it had bitten him. Of course John and I sympathized with him by laughing hysterically. That's the kind of thing that we all live for, abusing each other at hunting camp. I'm just glad that my first try on a mouth call was done in private …

A few years after that, Aaron was back at camp sounding better than me on a call, and armed with a shotgun. Our first morning out, with a gloom still settled in around us, we slowly worked the western part of the property. We were on an old logging trail in some fairly heavy hemlocks when a gobble sounded from the east fairly close. Aaron and John quickly got settled in by a pair of trees and I backed off a little and started to call. A pair of gobblers came in like they were on a string, walking right up to Aaron wearing signs that said, "Shoot me." I could see the heads bobbing around within fifteen or twenty yards of Aaron, and I was repeating, "Shoot!" over and over in my mind. The birds were just over a ridge from him, and as soon as one cleared he pulled the trigger. We were soon standing next to a very proud twelve year old with his first turkey. I guess that's the other thing we all live for at hunting camp.

From left to right, the author, Aaron Naklick and Dr. John Peebles following a great day of pheasant hunting.

To give you an idea of the kind of mind that's been influencing me all these years, here's an email John sent me after a normal day of turkey hunting:
> Imagine a morning where everything that can go wrong ... DOES! First off I set up on the ridge at 05:15, a perfect set up if I do say so myself ... well ... except for the fact that I set up right under the whole %$# damn flock. Imagine my surprise when they all flew down at the same time. They should have been a couple hundred

yards to the east ... but NO!!!! The other things that went wrong I would not really care to mention, like tripping and falling. Do you guys know how off center a fully packed XXL Turkey Vest makes you???

Anyways, I was just about to give up and pop a beer at 06:30 (AM that is) when a heard a couple of clucks from the field by my driveway. With all of the stealth that am not so famous for I snuck to the edge of my property and called this horny bastard and his two counterparts from 300+ yards out. They ran and gobbled and ran some more. Then they disappeared behind a knoll never to be seen again ... at least until they showed up 20 yards to my right ... yes right. So with my stealth I carefully switched my trusty 870 to my left arm only to find that I can't use my left eye ... it just wouldn't ##$$$%%$$# open. Anyways I got caught and a few warning puts later they were gone only to be called back by my oh-so-sexy Primos Box Call—talk about horny birds. So, again, moving with stealth I switched trees and picked out the biggest bird—recognizing him from an incident yesterday in which he beat the sh** out of a big gobbler that Aaron and I were bound to sucker in eventually—and shot him.

Chapter 3

Grouse Hunting 101
Late 1970's–Early 1980's

For the uninitiated, hunting grouse without the aid of a dog is a different type of sport. With a dog, you pretty much know where the birds are. Without a dog, it's something like walking through a poultry minefield. Every step is a potential explosion of noise and feathers. I'm convinced that the grouse know this and use it for their amusement. Don't believe me? Then why do they always flush when you're crossing a log with one leg in the air, one hand catching your hat, the other hand impaled on a thorn apple tree and the gun in your teeth?

How to properly react to a flushing grouse has probably been covered by guys with a lot more intelligence and shotgun shells than me, but I did spend quite a bit of my youth pursuing the little balls of fluff so I must admit that I feel a certain expertise in this area. My methods may differ slightly from the more refined bird man, but they've served me well through the years.

Standard procedure when a grouse explodes from the ground is to throw yourself in to the nearest pile of brush in case all that commotion at your feet is a skunk, snake, venomous wombat, etc. Next is to snap the gun to your shoulder and yank on the trigger. Direction is not important at this point, but your hunting partners would probably appreciate plus or minus forty-five degrees to the direction the bird is headed. Actually touching the gun to your shoulder is purely optional. Once you've got the warning shot out of the way, it's time to get serious. By now the grouse has accelerated to a point slightly under the speed of sound, and is bracing to break the barrier. You must quickly rack in another shell, slam the gun to your shoulder (no longer an option), swing twenty or thirty feet in front of the grouse and yank on the trigger again. Since the grouse will disappear into the foliage at exactly the moment your second shot is discharged, you can walk a few yards and take a look at how your gun is patterning.

There are of course alternative methods of scaring grouse, but they mostly involve alternatives like dropping the hammer on an empty chamber, or twisting a hundred and eighty degrees at the waist shooting backwards. A variation on the grouse's part is to explode from under your feet when you're on your way to a deer stand two hours before sunrise, when it's as dark as the inside of a cow. Proper procedure varies at this point since most game departments frown on warning shots at three in the morning. You still should dive into the nearest brush, since the venomous wombat is mostly nocturnal, but I always replace shooting with hyperventilation and heart palpitations.

Occasionally a grouse will flush ten or fifteen yards away from you instead of right under your feet. In this case, you no longer have to throw yourself into the nearest brush pile since you can immediately determine that you're out of immediate danger from skunks or venomous wombats. However, since they've got a head start on you, you must accelerate your actions accordingly. The first shot must be taken a split second after you hear the bird flush, the second can be taken at normal speed.

With this brief explanation of my grouse hunting methods firmly implanted in your mind, let me relate a little hunting episode that occurred while grouse hunting with Dr. Peebles. We were out behind his house walking the railroad tracks, and we were passing a stand of pines. The familiar sounds of a grouse busting out of cover radiated from the brush just to my left. Since there was no brush to jump into on the tracks and he was close to ten yards away, I skipped that part of the procedure and went right to the first shot. I followed the bird up and squeezed the trigger. Now, normally, when you hear a bird flush, by the time you get your gun to your shoulder the bird is out far enough to start shooting, even with that full choke JC Higgins.

In this case however, the bird had decided to come up out of the brush for a look around, or maybe a little exercise. I shot him just as he landed on a branch.... about eight yards away. To make matters worse, for once in my life I was dead on with my shot. There was an explosion of feathers like I had just hit a pillow truck. We walked over to investigate the scene with feathers still in the air, and started looking around. John deadpanned, "I think you hit him," as feathers gently settled on his shoulders. After quite a bit of searching, the only large chunk we found was the tail cut neatly at the base, ready for mounting. Now that is precision shooting!

Every so often you'll get the perfect flush. It will be in sparse cover, you'll catch the movement of the bird before he can scare you to death, and he'll fly straight away from you into the wind, rising slightly. This is called a "dream", wake up, because it never happens in real life. If by some chance this does happen, please let me know how you handled the situation. I've never had this happen, but I would imagine I would shoot five times in rapid succession slightly behind the bird to show him the error of his ways and to teach him a lesson about finding himself in such a compromising situation.

My most favorite grouse hunting is when there's snow on the ground. It's cool enough that you can dress so that you're not going to get overheated. You can actually track them sometimes as they walk along and put them out like a good bird dog. When the snow is just the right depth and consistency, grouse will burrow into it and nap contentedly. This is one of my most favorite ways to find them. Whether you track them to a hole in the snow, or you see the tell tale wing marks where they just dive bombed in, it's like finding a stash of gold. I normally sneak up on them and step in the general area of their den with my snowshoe or ski, and let them burst out of the snow in a flurry of feathers.

I was out back of my parents place one day on snowshoes and the snow was about a foot and a half deep. It was just fluffy enough to provide the perfect conditions for the grouse to burrow in, and I headed out eager to find them. Right at the beginning of the woods, I found some tracks wading through the deep snow, and then the tracks ended in a lump. On the far side of the lump was a clear sheen of ice about an inch square, where the grouse had been breathing. I stalked the bird like a cat, and managed to get right on top of it. I readied myself and thrust one snowshoe into the hole.

Whether the little bastard's directional sensor was broken or he came right up at my face on purpose I'll never know. I did what any reasonable person might do in that situation, I stepped backwards. Unfortunately, snowshoes don't come with a reverse gear, so I fell right on my back in the fluffy snow. At the same moment I made my strategic plummet, the grouse did a reverse gainer with a half twist and started clawing for air in the opposite direction. I had a great view of the acrobatics, being in the front row, so to speak.

Realizing I was down for the count, he flew directly away from me in a relatively open area. Not one to take that kind of behavior lying down (okay, I was), I swung on him from a reclined position, which everyone knows is nearly as steady as a prone position and took a shot at him. No, I didn't hit him, but I didn't blow my foot off either, so it was a win/win situation as far as I was concerned.

I was a pretty good cross country skier when I was younger, and when conditions were right, I'd head out on skis to grouse hunt. It was a faster mode of transportation to and from my hunting area, and once I'd start hunting I'd either drop off the poles at the edge of the woods, or carry them on my back. I was on skis one day on one of those perfect sunny winter days, where it's cold but there's no wind and the sun keeps you warm. I was going home after hunting for the morning, and I was headed down a hill in some sparsely brushed country.

I'm not sure exactly what happened, but as I was making my way down the hill, I kind of lost control. It was that kind of losing control where you don't fall down. You sort of lose your balance backwards, stand up straight, and fling your arms around in circles above your head. All the while this is happening you're picking up speed at an alarming rate.

It just so happened that there was a grouse on that same hill enjoying the sun, and when he caught sight of me bearing down on him, gesturing wildly, he panicked and flushed straight down the hill. By this time I had somewhat regained control, but was still moving along pretty good, and the timing was just right that I almost caught up to him enough to grab him by hand. Like a good quarterback, he felt the pressure on his back, kicked into another gear and pulled away. That was the only time I almost got a grouse without firing a shot.

We did get a woodcock once without firing a shot though. When I was about nine years old we got a part German Sheppard part Black Lab puppy that we named Kim. She was a very smart dog, and you could teach her just about anything you could think of. She knew each of us by name, could perform all the tricks and was extremely quick. Once we moved out into the country, we started taking her along periodically on our hunting trips. She quickly caught on that going for a walk in the woods was a lot of fun, and if you wanted her to go crazy all you had to do was rack a gun in the basement, and she'd be bouncing off the walls.

I was still too young to be carrying a gun and we had her across the road in thick cover. We put several grouse out of a thorn apple tree. That's all it took, she went around for the rest of that day looking up in all the trees. Even years later when I'd take her out, I'd catch her periodically checking out the trees.

We were in thick cover when she started looking birdie. A woodcock flushed and all of a sudden she leapt into the air and caught it about four feet off the ground. She presented it to my father and started looking for another just like nothing had happened. She stopped doing that kind of thing after I clued her in on that venomous wombat threat....

Chapter 4

First Deer
1979

With the lack of deer around my house during my teenage years, deer hunting was restricted to hunting my relative's land in central New York just off Keuka Lake. I had made the three hour drive to my grandparents every chance I could get in the fall. Following a frustrating year of airmailing slugs over a couple of deer due to inexperience, (or lack of intelligence) I was determined to fill my tag. I had hunted hard with a bow, and was seeing quite a few deer. One deer in particular had my attention. He was a nice two and a half year old eight point. To my young eyes he was a monster, and somehow I managed to see him almost every day.

It actually got to the point that I could predict his movements. To this day, I have never known a buck so well. There was an old cemetery on the side of a hill just off a vineyard with a strip of woods that served as a travel route for the buck. He also frequented a thick section of woods that led to another vineyard. I just could not seem to get a shot at him. I didn't realize how well I knew the buck until one day I was still hunting down by the cemetery and busted the buck out of there at close range. Without even thinking about it I took off on a dead run circling around on the route I knew he would take.

I stood panting at the edge of the woods with a knocked arrow on my bow peering into the thick cover. Just when I thought he had gone elsewhere I heard a branch crack fifty yards in. Then, antlers came floating into view. Unbelievably, that's all I could make out in the gloom. I had him at twenty yards several times, actually paralleling him for several yards, but in the thick cover, all I could ever make out were antlers. After perhaps five minutes of playing cat and mouse, he just vanished. I had no idea where he went, he could have just laid down for all I know.

Shotgun season came around, and I was shooting that old JC Higgins twelve gauge. Armed with a doe permit in hand I felt sure that this was my year to connect. My father and uncle took me to a large oak with a huge branch up about seven or eight feet in the air. They gave me a boost up there and with the words "Don't shoot a small one," they left me. It was a matter of a few short minutes when I saw movement and half expected that it was my uncle or father coming back for some reason. It wasn't, it was a doe and she was walking right up to me. My heart started pounding in my chest as I tried desperately to figure out how big she was. At five yards from me, I decided that she was big enough for me, aimed for her rib cage and pulled the trigger. She spun and ran off into the brush.

My uncle, who was just getting set up himself, heard the shot and came walking back over. I told him I had a deer down and he said something about finding a German Sheppard. Okay, so I shot a doe fawn, and maybe she wasn't the biggest deer in the world, but I was thrilled, I finally had taken a deer. There were jokes of course of not needing to drag it out, just grab it by a leg and carry it out like a rabbit. I had been known to give as well as receive, so I took it in stride and walked out of the woods on top of the world.

The next day found me with a buck tag still in my pocket and right back in the area where I had been seeing the eight point during bow season. I climbed up into a tree by the side of a vineyard and used a rope to bring my gun up. I was maybe twelve feet high sitting on a very small and especially uncomfortable branch. My father continued along to one of his favorite spots. I had seen nothing for a while when a barrage of shots erupted from the area around the cemetery. About five minutes went by when I realized there was movement in the vineyard, it was him! I had my gun up in a flash as the buck quickly walked down one of the rows of the vineyard, centered the sight on his chest and squeezed the trigger. He dropped in his tracks. I couldn't believe it, I had actually gotten him. I scrambled down the tree, stopping at the bottom to realize that my rope was still up there. I have no idea how I climbed down the branches with gun in my hand, but I did. I quickly reloaded just in case, and made my way over to the buck. He was huge, I was excited beyond words. My father was within shouting distance, so I yelled over to him that I had a buck down and pretty soon there were two idiots running around the vineyard.

Author with first deer on the right and first buck on the left.

We managed to get him gutted, and then kind of looked at each other when it came to getting him out of there, we were a long way from my grandparent's house. Dad found a pole and having seen it before in pictures, we decided to tie his legs to the pole and carry him out of there. We got him tied up and hoisted him up on our shoulders. It was incredible how much he weighed. After a short time we had him swinging so much he almost knocked me off my feet. It was time for a better idea, and dad suggested we go back to the house and see if we could bring the tractor up. My grandfather showed up in the tractor and we were back to the house in no time. That is definitely the best way to drag out a deer. So those were my first deer, and it marked a transition in me from being primarily a small game hunter, to that of a big game hunter.

Chapter 5

Bow Hunting is Easy
Late 1970's–1996

The nice year and a half old six point eased into my shooting lane on the crisp fall morning. I was perched on a small hill that gave me some cover and a good view of the surrounding brush and the vineyard just to my right. My heart wasn't pounding, I wasn't shaking, and the buck was only fifteen short yards away, feeding contentedly. I drew back the Pearson Shadow 100, a fearsome blend of state of the art technology and prehistoric ingenuity. The bow was set at a blistering sixty pounds and launched those heavy Bear arrows to within an inch of the bulls eye every single time.

Amazingly, I was brought to this point by a twenty pound bow that I found in the middle of the road. A friend and I were headed for Hardscrabble Bay on Lake Ontario, at that time some of the best small mouth fishing in the world. The cormorants and other invasive species have taken care of that since, but that's a subject for a whole different type of book. Something was lying in the road that we just managed to avoid. We stopped, and picked up a stick bow that had seen the wrong side of a few tires. When I got home, I got some cheap arrows and a hay bale from one of our neighbors. I found that I was actually a pretty good natural shot, and it was fun besides. That was the start of my bow hunting career.

As my interest grew, I went to a little better recurve bow, and then acquired the aforementioned Pearson Shadow 100. I put sights on the bow and was soon a very good shot due in large part to a great deal of punching hay bales. I got my first taste of bow hunting as a teenager when a neighbor agreed to take me out. He put me in a rickety tree stand in the middle of an open pine forest and told me he'd be back at dark to pick me up. I didn't see anything, but just being out in the woods with the thought of taking a deer with a bow cemented the desire to continue. All of this led me to a ground stand on my uncle's property in the southern part of New York facing that little six point.

I made the smoothest release ever and watched the arrow scream toward the unsuspecting buck. Then something happened. Something bad. The buck started to move, in slow motion. When the sound of the twanging bow reached the buck, he evidently made the immediate determination that he should quickly vacate the area rather than investigate. In order for the buck to spring away, he allowed his body to drop, and his legs to bend to implement maximum thrust to his limbs. Unfortunately for me, the timing of all this coincided exactly with the flight of the arrow reaching its intended mark, which turned out to be empty air. I now know that this is called "jumping the string". Back then, I called it something entirely different, not suitable for print.

I couldn't believe it as the buck sprinted away. Fortunately, he wasn't sure what had just happened and he made a quarter circle around me ending up in the vineyard only twenty five yards away. I quickly grabbed another arrow, drew back, put the twenty-five yard pin right behind his shoulder and released. The buck, having practiced the maneuver once, repeated it, and practically skipped away into the woods. I was never that calm on a buck ever again....

In fact that episode was the beginning of my contention that it was absolutely impossible to shoot a deer with a bow. I did absolutely everything wrong that you can possibly imagine. I had a doe right under my brand new baker tree stand once, perhaps three yards from the bottom of the tree. When I released, my lower limb hit a branch that I had not cleared. She darted away twenty yards and looked back to see what had spooked her. Unfortunately she was right behind a bush, but I could still see her grinning.

One day, I was sauntering across a swale field and a doe and buck popped up and stood broadside looking at me. He was a nice non-typical buck with a few stickers on his antlers standing at about thirty-five yards. Unfortunately for me, my range estimating abilities were somewhat deficient and I figured he was twenty-five yards away. Yup, one each arrow, delivered exactly to the point directly under his chest.

Another day, I had climbed up a tree in my Baker tree stand before first light. Back then, this procedure was accomplished by wrapping your arms around the tree and bringing your feet up, scraping the tree in the process. Then you brought your heels down locking the stand to the tree. It was a fairly slow noisy process and I liked to get it done very early to allow the woods to settle down afterwards. I had just put on my warm gear and was getting settled in when I happened to brush my bow with my arm. No big deal right? Well it wasn't except for the fact that my release was attached to the bow and I hit it perfectly on the thumb trigger. Down it went, disappearing into the gloom.

"Okay genius, now what are you going to do?" I thought to myself. Of course there was really only one thing to do. I dropped my bow back down to the ground, made my way noisily back down the tree and started looking for the release. And kept looking as the night turned to day. I finally found it and made my way back up the tree, again spooking everything within a quarter mile. I can't imagine why I didn't see anything that morning, but it did make me buy another release to put in my pack as soon as I got home. I've never dropped another one since, but there's always an extra in my pack.

A very tough lesson that I learned occurred late in the bow season one year. I had a Bear bow, which was set at seventy-three pounds. I had shot the bow all through the summer and into the fall. I had climbed into the stand an hour before sunrise with the temperature just above zero. I sat in the stand all day, dressed for about forty degrees. I wasn't especially bright back then, but I was in a spot that was a perfect funnel, and I just knew if I held out a buck would walk by at some point. The sun was just above the horizon preparing to disappear for the day, the temperature was dropping rapidly from the high of thirteen, and I was shivering like dachshund in a hot dog factory. A small buck was working his way down a trail that would pass within fifteen yards of me. I tried to stand once, and couldn't. The second try, I put a little more effort into it and managed to get to my feet. The buck stopped broadside, just where he was supposed to, and I drew the bow back.

No I didn't. I certainly gave it a good effort but it simply would not come back. Between the clothes I was wearing, and the hypothermia, the bow that I shot easily all summer long simply would not budge. I did finally heave it back, but all the commotion put the buck on alert and he escaped unscathed. The costly lesson I learned? Stay warm, or keep the bow at a poundage that cold muscles can handle.

I could probably write another book about all the other ways I messed up bow hunting when I was a kid, but I did finally manage to start putting it all together, after taking my first deer. I say "after", because my first deer with a bow was also a disaster. It was taken when I was still hunting. It was a relatively warm, sunny day and I was working my way very slowly through some heavy cover. A movement in front of me caught my attention and it soon materialized into a deer. With my bow hunting luck in the past, I had made the decision to take anything with legs that didn't "Moo" or "Meow". I mentally guessed the range at twenty yards and drew my bow back. Right after the release, I watched the flight of the arrow as it headed exactly toward the spot on the deer I was aiming. Then there was a cracking sound and the arrow dove to the ground right between the deer's feet. I had clipped an unseen dead branch about five yards in front of the deer. With my past experiences, I had gotten to the point where I almost expected things like this to happen.

The deer of course did not know that it was perfectly safe in front of me with a bow in my hands, and bolted to the right. To my surprise, in a few seconds it reappeared only about five yards further out, standing broadside. In slow motion I knocked another arrow and drew the bow back undetected. I knew that I would not hit the branch again since the deer was further away and the arrow's trajectory would take it over the branch. You guessed it, right into the branch again, except this time it hit the deer in the leg. I couldn't have felt worse. I tracked that deer throughout the day, losing the trail several times. By shear persistence I finally managed to finish the button buck off.

After that, I finally started to put all the pieces together. One deer that stands out is one that I took on Halloween. I was in my favorite tree stand on Fort Drum, a natural funnel in some thick cover. The only downside was that there were only a few small shooting lanes. It was a perfect evening to be in a tree stand, with cool temperatures and a steady breeze from the west. I knew that I had to hurry back to my house that evening because my three year old niece was coming to the house right after sunset. Don't worry, she wasn't driving, she was getting a ride from her parents.

It was about a half hour before sunset and I could hear a deer coming toward me moving fast. A rack appeared in the thick stuff as the deer came through at a fast walk. I had reached the point in my hunting career where I was starting to be a little selective on the bucks that I was taking so I wanted a decent look at the buck. He hit my first lane, I grunted and he never faltered, he just kept walking. I could see that he had a good frame to his rack, but that was about it. He headed for my second lane, and I decided to take him. I released the arrow at seventeen yards and it found the buck's lungs perfectly. He ran off and I heard the tell tale crash of him going down.

Knowing that I had a little visitor coming, I quickly tracked the buck and found that instead of the eight point I was expecting, he was a three and a half year old six point, but still a very nice buck. I was very happy with the exciting hunt, but now the sun was setting and I had a lot of work to do. I quickly gutted the buck and started dragging him back to the truck. Unfortunately, it was all up hill and by the time I got him up there I sounded like I was about to blow a gasket. I got him loaded into the truck and headed for the house. I pulled in just before my niece, who arrived dressed for Halloween, as a hunter.... perfect.

The author's niece Taylor Murtha with the Halloween buck.

Chapter 6
Saskatchewan Silver Tip
1990

As time progressed, and I got more skilled as a hunter, it got to the point where I could fill my tag at the beginning of each season. Deer hunting was becoming too easy, too short and not as satisfying. I decided one year that I would let any young bucks walk. It was early in bow season and I was bow hunting from a tree stand on a cool fall evening. A sound in the leaves became a deer and then a buck. A year and a half old six point was headed my way. I stayed glued to my seat, just watching him saunter along. As he walked by at an easy twenty yards and then away, the world didn't come to an end, I didn't burst into flames or anything like that, and best of all I was still hunting. That one incident started an entirely different view of hunting for me. Call me a trophy hunter if you like, but I'd rather be out in the woods than sitting on the couch, and this is the best way to do it. On top of that, to me there's nothing better than seeing a big mature buck in the woods. The only way to do that is to let him go when he's a dumb youngster.

New York's management of the deer herd is and always has been somewhat questionable. The buck to doe ratio is way out of kilter, and the overwhelming majority of bucks are killed when they're a year and a half old. Unlike the western states, everyone with a pulse gets a tag, and there are a lot of hunters. It's quite a feat to take an older buck unless you've got a large chunk of private land that you can control. It's too bad because in many areas the food and genetics are there to consistently produce world class bucks. My cousin took a 4x4 buck one year that probably would score right around a hundred points. We took it to a check station and found that it was actually only a year and a half old. I just shake my head when I think of what a buck like that could be at five and a half years old. Those kinds of genetics are running around all over New York, if they could only get a chance to show themselves. Unfortunately in most areas, if a hunter sees antlers, the lead starts flying.

Growing up in that environment, I had spent years reading about the big bucks taken in other areas of the country, or up in Canada. I finally decided that if I wanted to see really big bucks I needed to get out of New York. So, I started saving money each paycheck in anticipation of going on an outfitted hunt somewhere far away. Once I was financially set I contacted agent Collins Kellogg and he said that a person he knew from Alberta was going to set something up with an outfitter in Saskatchewan. The price was right and I soon had my deposit headed for Canada. I knew it was going to be cold, so with help from the family at Christmas I got some Mickey Mouse boots and other various cold weather gear. The way it turned out, they should have another word for "cold" up there, because that word just doesn't cover it.

The time passed quickly and soon I was on an airplane headed for Saskatoon. The flight was smooth and my luggage actually made the trip with me, which is always a plus. I was shortly picked up by Fred Wilkening from Alberta and Saskatchewan outfitter Garry Debienne who owned Silver Tip Outfitters up near Tobin Lake. Along with renting some cabins on the lake, he primarily outfitted for fishing and some waterfowl hunting. This was his first shot at outfitting for deer. I stepped out in to the parking lot and the cold hit me like a wall. It was the kind of cold that got your immediate attention. Being from northern New York I was very familiar with cold temperatures, but normally during hunting season the temperature would not drop below zero Fahrenheit. I'm not sure how cold it was, but I was very happy to jump into the van for the trip north.

I learned that Fred was originally from Germany and had guided for sheep and deer in the past. Garry had lived in the wilds of Alberta for a while and was a top notch fishing guide. We pulled in to one of Garry's cabins, threw our stuff into the rooms and got settled in. There ended up being seven of us in camp for the hunt. The next day was Sunday, and hunting is not allowed. I was introduced to my guide Dean and we went for a little drive. The cabin was in an area where nonresident hunting was not allowed and it was about an hour drive around the lake. We looked over some of the country we were going to be hunting. Then we headed back to make sure our rifles were still on and to prepare for the hunt.

I awoke the first morning and looked in disbelief at the thermometer. The mercury was dipping beneath the twenty below zero mark. I couldn't believe we were actually going to go outside at that temperature, and stay there....

on purpose. So I loaded up enough clothing for an arctic expedition and we headed out into the darkness. We started with some still hunting through the bush almost losing one person in the process as he veered off the correct heading. The area we were hunting was very remote, to the point that if you headed north you probably would see polar bears before another human being. I definitely paid attention to my compass after that. Later, some stand hunting was tried, and some drives were made, all with limited success. The first day passed with me seeing just a few does. I wasn't wild about the drives we were putting on, so I elected to do some still and stand hunting the next day.

The next morning we saw a good buck dash into some bush and I spent the morning in a tree stand nearby without seeing a hair. The other guys continued to try drives with some success. One of them wounded a buck and they tracked it for quite some time. During the afternoon we all teamed up to see if we could find the buck. He had run onto a piece of property we didn't have permission to hunt, so Garry contacted the landowner and got permission for us to track the buck onto the property without firearms. I was placed on the road to see if the buck busted out of there, and several of the guys went in on the track. In about ten minutes I saw motion in the bush. A hundred forty class whitetail burst out of there and crossed the road about twenty yards in front of me. I stood there with my mouth open watching that monster run across the field. He was the biggest buck I had ever seen on the hoof, and you might say that I was impressed.

It turned out that the wounded buck had crossed the road several hours before, and there were coyote tracks on the trail. Nothing that's bleeding lasts very long up in the wilds of Saskatchewan. The buck was tracked further, but the blood stopped and he was lost when his tracks intermingled with some other deer. After the search was halted Garry and Dean took some of the guys to several thousand acres of dense bush. One of them even had an encounter with a monster buck, which escaped hole free after a few shots. I decided to join them and I went back in along some old gas exploration trails over two miles back in the bush and found a spot that seemed like it should funnel the deer around a beaver pond. I had been sitting there for a short time when there were several shots in front of me and then some yelling. One of the guys had taken some shots at a buck that was running across a beaver dam. That's not what the yelling was about though. He had found a buck that may have been killed in a fight that was as beautiful a typical twelve point as you'd ever want to see, probably pushing Boone and Crockett.

I left the bush that evening with visions of monster bucks dancing in my head. The next day, we left early in the minus twenty five degree morning and headed back to the same area. I dressed very light despite the temperature, for the fifty minute forced march ahead of me. I had loaded up my pack to the bursting point and then strapped another twenty pounds or so of clothing to the outside, intending to spend the day. Once we arrived at the edge of the bush Dean dropped me off and I headed back into the bush, with the snow squeaking under my feet. I had walked about twenty minutes when I saw some different looking tracks on the trail. With the snow on the ground, it was light enough to walk without a light so I wasn't really sure what I was looking at. My first thought from the size of them was that they were bear tracks. I knew that no bear in his right mind would still be wandering around at that time of year, so I dug out my flashlight to take a better look. I turned on the light and found myself looking at the biggest canine track I'd ever seen in my life. They were a set of wolf tracks the size of my extended hand. I could not believe how big they were.

With a quick look around to see if I was being sized up for breakfast I continued down the trail. I reached my designated tree and dumped my pack on the ground. I had gotten a little overheated, so I waited a bit to cool down then I started putting on clothes until I had so much on I could barely bend my arms, or anything else for that matter. I slid on my Icebreaker insulated over boots over my Mickey Mouse boots and placed my foam seat on the ground and sat down to await sunrise.

Sunrise didn't look a lot different than the dead of night. Dull steel gray clouds drifted low overhead and a light snow drifted lazily down. I concentrated on sitting still and trying to stay warm. A few hours had passed when there was movement in the bush in front of me. A very tall but narrow eight point walked out on the trail twenty yards away and stood there staring at the big strange looking stump in front of him. I guessed him to be three and a half years old, and while he was a nice buck, easily the biggest I would have ever shot, I decided to pass. If he had popped out on the first day I would have taken him, but after what I had seen, I was looking for something a little bigger.

The buck got nervous and trotted down the trail with his ears pinned back, listening to see if I was pursuing him. Little did he know I could barely move. Eventually he wandered back into the bush and I was left to count snowflakes. About mid morning it was very still and I thought I heard a noise in the thick willows in front of me. Several minutes went by and I figured I must have been mistaken. Then, I heard a click of what to me was an antler clipping a branch. That feeling was so strong that I pulled my hands out of my muff and put the gun to my shoulder with the muzzle pointed at the ground in front of me. I caught movement a split second before the buck broke out of the cover directly in front of me at perhaps thirty yards. I've never made such a quick decision in my life, I took one look at the rack and brought the rifle up and snapped off the safety. He caught the movement and stopped quartering toward me just as I centered the scope and squeezed the trigger.

At the shot, the buck bolted back into the brush. I listened for the telltale crash, but heard absolutely nothing. I sat there shaking like a leaf, and doubt started to creep in. I ran the shot in my mind a dozen times. There's no way I could have missed at that range. I waited for what seemed like hours, but was probably no more than twenty minutes and went to look for some sign. I found just a few strands of hair where the buck had been standing and I started tracking the massive bounds of the buck. There must have been some rutting activity in the area before I arrived in the morning because there were running tracks everywhere. The snow was so light and fluffy, and he was taking such large bounds, it was hard to tell which tracks belonged to the buck. I had gone at least fifty yards on the tracks that I thought were his and had not come up with a single speck of blood in the snow. Knowing that he should be bleeding freely by then, I backtracked and reworked the trail. I must have wandered around in there for at least half an hour, becoming more and more convinced that I somehow missed the buck of a lifetime.

I began making circles a little further out into the bush trying to pick up a blood trail when I walked right into him. I saw the brown lump in front of me and cautiously approached, but there was no need, he was done. I lifted that massive rack out of the snow and couldn't believe it. He was so much bigger than anything I had ever had my hands on I was dumbstruck. He was a typical 5x5 with long tines and an eighteen inch inside spread.

Backtracking the buck, I had come within twenty yards of him a few times, but could not see him in the thick brush. I had been on his track several times, and he did not leave a drop of blood. The bullet had entered in the right front shoulder and had angled to the back left leg, with no exit wound. Then, I was struck with the sensation that I really didn't want to leave the buck, but I had to go get Dean who was sitting by a nice fire at the edge of the bush. I packed up my equipment and started practically running down the trail. It took forever to get out, but I finally hit the edge of the bush. I could see a few trucks and people sitting around a fire about four hundred yards away.

Author and guide with the big Saskatchewan whitetail.

I couldn't seem to get anyone's attention, whistling, hollering and jumping up and down like a mad man. I finally just sighed and started walking over. Someone noticed me when I was about half way there and Dean jumped into his truck and came over to see what was going on. I gave him the story, and he seemed almost as excited as me about the buck. We got Garry and a snowmobile, and headed back into the bush. Half expecting the buck to be gone, I took them into the area and I could tell that they were happy with the buck as well. After we admired the buck for a while, we dragged him to the trail. We tied the deer to the back of the sled, and headed for the trailhead.

We loaded him into the back of the truck and headed into town to a local meat cutter that had a scale. The buck was pretty worn down from the rut, and was all shoulders and neck. His hindquarters looked like a greyhounds. We pulled him up on the scale, and it settled on two hundred five pounds dressed weight. I can't imagine how much he would have weighed early in the season. Back at camp, we put a tape to the buck, and while numbers don't mean much to me, I was astonished when we came up with a hundred and fifty four and 5/8 inches on a clean ten point. I could have hunted a lifetime in New York without even seeing a buck of that caliber.

What could be better than shooting a big buck? Having a second tag in my hand. The next morning had me repeating my trek back into the bush in the frigid darkness. I got all my gear on and sat by the tree, to await another sunrise. As night turned to day a group of coyotes opened up a half mile away, and pretty soon it sounded like there were coyotes everywhere. I doe nervously skittered past me with her ears tucked back. She wanted nothing to do with that group. They finally quieted down, and the woods returned to silence. Then a crash sounded off in the distance in the heavy willow thickets. That was soon followed by another. Something was headed my way at a fast clip. I heard the tell tale sound of a grunting buck as the deer swung past my position in the thick stuff and then headed away again. Pretty soon they were on their way back, but further down the trail. I trotted down, paralleling the sound the best I could but they turned away again and headed back into the bush.

I had just started back to my tree when I heard them circling for another run. A doe burst across the opening, running full speed eighty yards away. I knew what was coming and that I'd have to make a split second decision. I decided that if I could see a rack, I'd take the shot. The buck sailed into the opening after the doe. My rifle was already to my shoulder and I immediately saw a good bit of bone on his head. In slow motion the crosshairs caught up to the buck and settled perfectly on the hairline of his chest as he made a leap across the clearing. I dropped the hammer, the gun thumping against my shoulder through the thick clothing, and the buck was gone.

I waited a little while and walked up to where the deer had crossed. With an outcome exactly the opposite of the previous buck, there was a red carpet leading into the bush. I walked right to the buck, and was satisfied with a nice nine point. The shot had taken the top of the heart, and he went perhaps fifty yards before dropping. As before, I walked out and told Garry that the same thing happened to this buck as the last one, there was absolutely no blood trail. He talked to me pretty hard when he saw the red carpet, but it was worth it to see the look on his face when he saw it.

We dragged the buck out and got him taken care of, and I reflected on the events of the past few days. The experience changed my perspective on hunting forever. There really were places where the buck to doe ratio was good, the bucks could live to maturity and the woods weren't filled with orange. I vowed then and there that this would not be my last out of state hunting trip, and to a great extent that trip shaped much of my future.

Chapter 7
Broken Leg Buck
1991

It was a beautiful crisp fall day in northern New York. I had spent the morning perched in a tree with a bow in my hand. I was preparing to hike into the Adirondack Mountains in a few days for the opening of the muzzle loading season, and needed a few supplies in town. Since it was such a nice day, I decided to jump on my motorcycle for the trip. I was moseying along at about forty-five mph minding my own business when a black cat dashed out of the ditch line into the road right in front of me. My immediate reaction was to hit the front brake, to be followed post haste by the rear brake. The first part of the plan worked fine, until the wheel stopped spinning and started skidding. Spinning apparently maintains some sort of traction with the pavement, and when the spinning stops, the traction does also. The end result was the bike landing on its side, and I started my own brand of spinning. I ended up bouncing along on my elbows and knees with every rotation. That actually would have been fine, except that the bike decided to keep pace with me and I was beating my legs on the gas tank. Yes, "Ouch"....

I distinctly remember a cracking sound and was aware at one point of a shoe flying off one of my feet. I stopped rolling after a while and started to take stock of my various parts. It appeared that everything was still attached, but I was pretty sure both of my legs were broken. By the time the medics arrived I had decided that maybe only one of them was broken. As they started to lift me onto the gurney, there was definitely some excessive flopping going on that was fairly uncomfortable. I asked them if they might immobilize the leg before we continued. They did so, and I was treated to a ride to the hospital, complete with sirens blaring.

Several hours later I had a plate in my leg and a morphine trigger in my hands. As if that wasn't bad enough, I was scheduled for a return trip to Saskatchewan in less than two months. I talked to my doctor about it and while he didn't seem overly optimistic, he said we'd see how everything went. I had broken the tibia just above the ankle at an odd angle, and the fibula up by my knee. The fibula looked like it had been crushed since it was nothing but fragments for about an inch.

I spent six weeks on crutches with absolutely no pressure on the leg. Less than a week before my trip, my Doctor decided that he could put a walking cast on and I could begin to put some weight on the leg. I retreated to my camp in central NY for rehab, and maybe a little bow hunting. Just before I left, coworker Denise Walker showed up to work with a pair of camouflaged crutches, so I was ready to go.

I started putting weight on the leg little by little. Every time I did, it felt like there were a thousand pins in the bottom of my foot and the screws in the plate were pulling out of the bone in my leg. With the urgency of the trip, I forced the issue and ignored the pain. In two days I was walking with a cane (well, a sand wedge), and by the time it was time to head for Canada I was putting my full weight on the leg, but I had virtually no strength in it.

I had an interesting time going through airport security, but I managed to convince everyone that the cast was real and I wasn't carrying anything dangerous inside my leg. Garry Debienne met me at the airport. As he watched me limp toward him he just shook his head, probably thinking that I was slightly off my rocker to be there, but willing to give it a try. We got caught up with each other and soon I was settled in and ready to go.

My first day out, Garry took me to a ground blind that was only a little over a hundred yards into the woods. It was about ten below zero F and there was a foot of snow on the ground. It was also my first experience walking in the snow with basically no right ankle. Ever think about just what your ankle does when you're walking through the woods? Nope, me neither, until the moment I stepped on something under the snow and just flopped over. The look on Garry's face when he turned around was priceless as I floundered around like a carp out of water. We managed to get me back on my feet and continued on, this time with me in the lead. I hit another bump and started to fall, when Garry caught me. He figured with a little support, I could right myself, but on that leg, once I started over I might as well yell "Timber!" He ended up having to get his feet under him and pretty much leg pressing me back into place. We both ended up laughing so hard that it was some time before we could proceed. For the rest of the hunt, I ended up with a face full of snow more times than I'd like to admit. I saw a few deer the first day but no shooters. I really didn't care, I was just glad to be out there.

The second day was an experience I won't soon forget. Garry took me to an area that his previous hunters had seen some decent bucks a few weeks earlier. The bad news was that there was a mile walk just to get to the wood line. The worse news was that it was the coldest day I had seen in Canada. To this day, I don't remember ever looking at the thermometer, put it was noticeably colder than anything I had ever experienced. Since I'd been out several times at less than minus twenty degrees F, I would guess that it was well into the minus thirties. The walk out was endless, with me having all the physical prowess of a man who spent two months on the couch eating Cheetos. My cast was gnawing a hole in my shin, and every part of my body was trying to turn into an icicle. I spent the morning alternately still hunting when I got cold, and sitting once I got warmed up. I didn't see any deer, but did see a large set of moose tracks. I normally don't mind spending the day in the woods, but I was back in the van around lunch time to recover a bit.

We discussed the lack of deer sign, and decided to head for a different area in the afternoon. He explained where it was and dropped me off by the side of the road. I spent the next ten minutes trying to crawl up the bank the snowplow had left. I finally made it into the woods and ended the day with only a few doe sightings.

The next morning found me back in the ground blind before sunrise. The blind was on a small ridge that you would hardly notice, but the deer liked to walk along the ridge on the edge of some spruce trees and thicker brush. It was very still when I went in, but shortly the wind started to pick up. I didn't like the direction, so I changed locations shortly after day break. About mid morning, it paid off. I caught some movement out of the corner of my eye fifty yards out, and a beautiful 5x5 stepped out of the thick stuff. I didn't even hesitate, as soon as his head went behind some brush I snapped the gun to my shoulder. Once he cleared, I squeezed the trigger and he dropped in his tracks.

I limped over to the buck and admired the heavy fur, thick neck and great rack of a mature northern whitetail. I also felt a sense of accomplishment, being able to overcome the lack of mobility.

Following a very brief rehab with a walking cast, the author took this fine Canadian buck.

It took me a while to walk back to my spot, take off my heavy clothing, and get everything in my pack. Then I took some more time to make it to the road. Garry had happened to be just down the road and had heard the shot and was waiting for me. I walked up to the van and just shook my head. He asked what happened and I told him that I had pulled the shot and blew snow up in front of a nice buck. He indicated that he had actually started in to the bush, but held up when he didn't see any sign of me. After a while he returned to the van. I finally let him off the hook and told him there was a nice buck lying in there and he said something derogatory about my ancestry that was totally uncalled for.

We managed to get a snowmobile back in close to the buck and dragged him out. Back at his place, we grabbed some more pictures and joked about which limb I was going to break the following year. We had some time to kill, so we decided to take his van and drive some of the back roads around his house. We had seen a few deer, but nothing very big when a horse with antlers burst out of the brush right in front of the van. Garry slammed on the brakes, and I grabbed my camera and leapt out of the van. I grabbed some pictures, but they don't do the buck justice. He was a typical five by five, with a monstrous body, which made his antlers almost appear normal on his head. I figured he was a Booner for sure. Did I mention we were in an area I couldn't hunt? That's very painful....I wonder what it would take to become a Canadian Citizen?

Chapter 8
Solo in Montana
1992 & 1995

A red squirrel was happily chattering away a hundred yards into the woods, scolding something in his imagination or something that was really moving through his territory. I heard a noise around the side of the little hill I was on and swung around to look just as a set of antlers poked above the grass. The buck was coming right towards me and was close enough that I didn't dare move. My rifle was sitting beside me, and might have well have been ten feet away. I was sitting there in anticipation of a shot down below me at several hundred yards, not having a deer walk right over me. The buck finally realized that something was up at about five yards and bolted down the slope, spraying dirt in my face in the process.

I was sitting on a hillside in the Kootenai National Forest west of Kalispell Montana on a beautiful sunny fall day in November. I had hunted solo many times in the wilderness areas in the Adirondack Mountains, packing a tent in and spending several days in pursuit of whitetails. In 1992 I found myself somewhat short of funds to head back to Saskatchewan, but I still wanted to experience a hunt in another part of the world. I researched the public land available in Montana through several different sources and put in for a combination elk/deer tag. Luck was with me and I drew the tag. Prior to the hunt I prioritized several different areas that could produce elk and either whitetail or mule deer.

I left upstate New York about noon on a nice fall day and headed west in my trusty pickup truck. I passed by Chicago at about midnight, which I've found is about the only time there isn't a traffic jam. I kept going until about three am, pulled into a rest stop, and climbed in to the back of the truck for some sleep. I slept for a few hours and hit the road again at about six thirty. Did I mention I was young and dumb? I drove till about two in the morning and again headed for the back of the truck. I hit the road in the morning and pulled into Kalispell sometime during the middle of the day. I found a hotel, got cleaned up and headed out to look over the area I selected first, which was south of Kalispell. I ended up not even getting out of the truck, but I did find a likely looking spot to start first thing the next morning.

Not being familiar with the area, I waited until it started to get light before I headed in to the snow covered woods. I had only gone a short distance when I saw brown movement against the white background. I nice ten point buck probably scoring around a hundred and thirty points stepped out in front of me. "Great, now what do I do?" I thought to myself. Did I really drive for forty-one hours to shoot a buck within minutes of beginning my hunt? The answer turned out to be no, but he really was a nice buck. I continued on without seeing anything further. I found an area where there was a gate across the trail to restrict vehicular traffic, and several hills and draws in the region beyond. I decided to set up camp and explore the area. In this case, setting up camp pretty much meant that I parked my truck.

The next morning I walked in about a half mile in the predawn darkness to look the area over. I decided to sit for a while in the morning looking at a hillside. Everything went fine until a red squirrel saw me. He came over, sat above my head and chattered at me. This seemed to go on forever, and it looked like he didn't need to even breathe. I finally had had enough and decided I was going to spook him out of there. I stood and waived my arms at him, which just increased the decibel level of his displeasure. Well, that did it for me, he was going to have to leave, period. I packed a snowball and threw it at him. He dodged to one side, went further up the tree and really let me have it. Several snowballs later, I walked away, completely defeated by the little devil.

I wandered around for the day and didn't see anything except a few flags. As sunset approached the sky opened up and started spitting snow pellets. I decided to still hunt my way back to the truck. I had not gone far when I ran into several sets of elk tracks that were so fresh there were just a few of the pellets in the tracks. It looked to me like they were from a calf, two cows and a big bull. I jumped on the tracks and followed for about a half mile, trying to catch up to them. As darkness approached I finally had to abandon the trail and head for the truck. I was a hundred yards from the truck, when I saw the same sets of tracks cross the trail and again they were only minutes ahead of me. What I would have given for another hour of daylight at that point.

I hunted the same area the next day seeing just a few does and a small buck. I decided to change locations. After spending the night in Kalispell I headed for the Kootenai. I took special interest in the sign on the way in to the area that told me how to tell the difference between a black bear and a grizzly bear. I found a spot that gave me access to public land all around and parked. With camp all set up, I set out for a little exploration. There was a big mountain across the road that held the promise of mule deer and elk. There was a stream running just the other side of the road with some thick cover that suggested perfect whitetail habitat with thick cover and several drainages on my side of the road. There was also a power line running adjacent to the road with some clearings that I might be able to make use of. I found rubs and scrapes, and quickly put together the pieces to establish where the major deer activity was.

For the next several days I hunted that area, seeing four nice bucks in the one twenty class, but I let them all go. I was enjoying the area too much to let it end prematurely. One day I climbed up on top of the mountain, but only saw a few whitetails. That evening I was cooking dinner on the tailgate of the truck. All of a sudden about a hundred yards into the woods there was a sound of a knock down drag out fight between two animals with claws, teeth and bad attitudes. A pair of mountain lions were tearing the place apart. The hair went up on the back of my neck as I stared into the gloom. The fight lasted for quite some time and sounded ferocious. The only thing worse than listening to them go at it was when the noise stopped. I've never had problems being in the woods at night, but the eerie feeling that accompanied that sudden silence was as intense as any I've ever felt. With two big kitty cats wandering around out there with hurt feelings, I decided it was a good time to turn in for the night.

As my hunting time quickly dwindled I decided to spend a good part of a particularly nice sunny pleasant day overlooking the opening for the power line from an adjacent hillside. There were numerous trails that ran in front of me and I had seen several deer in the area, so I got set up and settled in. This takes us back to the start of the story when the eight point tried to walk over me. He wasn't the biggest buck I had seen by far, but time was short and he was still a nice buck. He ran down the hill and stopped at about a hundred and twenty yards out, turning to see what the heck he had walked into. As he was running I had grabbed the rifle, and was on him when he stopped. I placed the crosshairs behind his shoulder and squeezed the trigger. He dropped in his tracks. I found a place to get the meat processed and frozen in Kalispell, and spent the next day taking pictures and half heartedly looking for an elk. After getting the meat processed, I was back on the road for the long trip home, having enjoyed the experience immensely.

After a great week of hunting, the author took this nice 4x4 in Montana.

Three years later, after my father retired, I got him to take a trip back to the same area. This time however we stayed in hotels on the way out, and I had acquired a nice roomy outfitter tent to stay in. After a fairly uneventful trip out, we headed back to the same area with the power line. There were several inches of snow on the ground so we cleared an area the best we could and set up camp. With cats and two brands of bears in the area, I asked dad how it felt to be a couple rungs down on the food chain. I could tell that he suddenly looked at that thin tent from a different perspective, and I think he muttered something about how solid hotel room walls were.

It had only been a few years between trips, but I was astonished at how much the trees and brush had grown up on the power line right of way. The hillside that I had been on when I shot the eight point offered practically no visibility what so ever anymore. Over the next several days we hunted the area hard as temperatures generally warmed during the days and the snow melted. Neither one of us was seeing much. I did see what I felt was a good buck at a scrape, but early morning light and fogged glasses made him fuzzy enough that I didn't shoot. The bucks simply weren't running the way they had during the earlier trip, though the reason evades me to this day.

Nights in the tent were interesting, with clearing skies producing quite a drop in temperatures down into the single digits. There's nothing like getting out of a nice warm sleeping bag at four thirty in the morning to really get the blood pumping. It seems like perhaps my father had a different feeling on the matter, although it was hard to understand the muffled comments he was making from inside the sleeping bag.

We were almost out of hunting days and I decided to hunt down by the stream. I got settled into a spot with some good sign all around. I hadn't been there too long when I heard brush crashing to my right. A deer came right at me at a dead run. As the doe skidded past me a few feet away I could hear a second deer bulldozing through the brush behind her. The buck broke cover and I could see a rack on his head. As he ran past I grunted loudly at him and he skidded to a halt about twenty yards away. I shot him through the shoulders and he went down a short distance away.

I headed back to camp and found my father there waiting for me. He had heard the shot and came to the logical conclusion that I had a buck down. I told him about the hot doe and we decided that he should spend the rest of the day down there on the same trail. We quickly got my buck out of there, got my father settled in and left the area. As the sun set, he came up the hill to camp. He had not seen a thing after I left. I tried to offer encouragement, since there was still another day left to hunt, but he made an executive decision and said that the hunt was over and it was time to leave. He didn't mean in the morning, either. I guess the prospect of spending another night in a sleeping bag with the temperature hovering around single digits didn't fill him with a great deal of enthusiasm.

So as darkness fell, we tore down camp, packed up the truck and headed for a nice warm hotel, with a nice hot shower. Some people have no sense of adventure.

Chapter 9
Frozen in Saranac
1993

The temperature was dropping, the wind was howling, snow squalls were screaming through the area and I was a long way from home. Where was I? On the wrong side of Saranac Lake in the Adirondack Mountains of New York and it was mid November.

A good part of the Adirondacks are hard hunting. Most of the forests are old growth, since any kind of logging is apparently viewed as something akin to kicking puppies. The undergrowth is practically nonexistent and much of the area is fairly devoid of life. As far as I can tell, a good part of the deer herd up there survives most of the winter by eating snowballs. The deer population in the high peaks region is generally low, but there are a few good bucks that are taken each year. I had spent a good part of a summer trying to find public land in the mountains that was hard to get to, in order to find some bucks with some age. I came up with the brilliant idea of canoeing across the Middle Saranac Lake, and camping on the other side. I figured there weren't too many people that would go to that much trouble, and I was right. There's apparently a reason for that.

The first year I went up there, I invited a friend of mine, Jim Reape. We took two canoes, one electric motor, plenty of waterproof matches and headed across. I was disappointed to find a few other tents, but we found an area to ourselves, saw a few deer and generally had a good time. We did head back a bit early when we heard on the radio that some bad weather was moving in, but the whole trip went off without a hitch.

The following year, Jim evidently was feigning intelligence or made up some kind of an excuse so I headed across on my own. There were no other hunters in there, with one tent set up for future use. The first day I saw a big deer disappear up a mountain, but couldn't put horns on it. I also saw a doe being pursued by a coyote. On the way back to camp that evening I stumbled across a shed antler from the previous year that had good mass, and long thick tines. If the other side matched, he'd be a buck in the one forties, a very good buck for the area. From the mass alone, I guessed the buck to be at least five years old, a very rare buck in New York on public land.

A few more days passed, a few more deer were seen, but no shooters. I had a radio with me and always listened to the weather report....except for one night. The wind started to pick up in the middle of the night and it wasn't long when the sound of trees crashing to the ground echoed through the darkness above the howling of the wind. When you're stuck in a tent, in the woods, crashing sounds of any kind are generally not welcomed with great enthusiasm. It got to the point where I was wondering if there were going to be any trees still standing by the time morning rolled around. I somehow survived the night, and as soon as it started to get light I broke camp.

I was back into a small offshoot of the main lake, and I had to travel perhaps half a mile to hit the main body of water. I got everything loaded into the canoe, fired up the electric trolling motor and headed for home at flank speed, which in this case was something like the speed of a wounded golf cart. Everything was fine until I hit the main lake and launched myself into the teeth of the wind. I was barely making headway and the waves were huge frothy walls of gray slamming into the boat. I decided very quickly that it was probably not a good day to take a swim, since I had not brought my swimming trunks, so I figured I'd head back to shore. Okay, the decision had been made, so the only thing left was the actual execution. The "turning around" maneuver was going to be very interesting. I tried to just turn the motor around 180 degrees and head right back in, but the wind caught the bow and started to whip me around sideways. That was a bad thing. I basically waited for a few waves that weren't over my head, and cranked the boat around as quickly as possible. I got closer to doing the breaststroke than I like to admit, but I soon made a rough landing on the icy shore.

The temperature kept dropping, the squalls kept rolling through and if anything the wind actually increased. I decided to wait out the weather till three pm, and if it didn't break, I'd set up camp on the shore. Three o'clock came and went, and I started to pull everything out of the canoe. The big question became how on earth do you set up an outfitters tent in a hurricane without becoming a kite? Well, the answer is that you stand there and stare at the tent in its bag for a while hoping for some kind of inspiration. When that doesn't happen, you dump it out and start staking the bottom into the wind and kind of work the tent into the air from the bottom up. A healthy dose of swearing is not only recommended, it's required.

Not everyone can say they used a canoe as an ice breaker.

After another wild night, I awoke to an eerie dead calm. I had learned a long time ago that an expensive sleeping bag inside a cheap sleeping bag would keep me comfortable in just about any conditions, but I could tell that the temperature had continued to plummet. I shined a flashlight around the tent and found that my bottle of soda was frozen solid. I broke camp in the predawn darkness and hit the water as soon as I could see the far shoreline. Instead of going directly across the lake, I made a wide arc, paralleling the shoreline. I noticed that there was ice all the way around the shore, sometimes covering several hundred feet into the lake. As I approached the half mile of feeder stream that I had to traverse I knew that my day was far from over.

The stream was solid ice, of perhaps an inch thickness. I briefly thought of carrying everything back to my truck along the bank of the stream, but the cover was very thick and swampy. I let the bow nudge up onto the edge of the ice and after a few feet it broke through. That was interesting, so I backed up and tried it again. It worked again, except that this time the prop started grinding on the ice that I had broken off the first trip. I immediately shut the motor down, convinced that I had just shattered the blades. To my surprise, the blades were intact. I started using a paddle to pole my way up on the ice but it was apparent that I was fighting a losing battle. I decided to use the motor until I broke the prop and then deal with the situation.

I used the paddle in combination with "the grinder", and made my way slowly up the stream. Half a day later found me wearily stepping out of the boat at the boat launch. I felt like kissing the ground.... and my truck ... and the cute blond hiker standing by her Jetta.

I didn't shoot a deer during that hunt, but it's definitely one of my most memorable adventures. It's a stark reminder to pay attention and be prepared when you're out of touch with civilization.

Chapter 10

Oxygen, it's a Good Thing
1993–Present

We drove as far as we could up the mountain and parked precariously on the slope. I jumped out of the jeep into the cold crisp air at just under ten thousand feet. The sky was clear and the wind was brisk. I started up the slope behind All Pro Rulon Jones and was gasping like a carp after about thirty yards. I could not believe it. I was thirty years old, in good shape, and I was breathing like I had been doing wind sprints for ten minutes.

If you read the books that are provided by so called experts on the subject, you'll find that the effective oxygen concentration at sea level is 20.9%, and 14.2% at ten thousand feet above sea level. Those numbers are all wrong. While I may not have taken any scientific equipment up on the mountains, I can tell you from experience that at ten thousand feet, oxygen levels drop to .01%. It gets to the point where if you see an oxygen molecule float by, you grab it and put it in your pocket for later use. I use my extra oxygen molecules when my guide insists on sprinting a hundred yards up a shear cliff just to see what's on the other side. Even so, I could never see what was on the other side anyway, because it's hard to glass laying on my back gasping for air.

I was hunting mule deer with Rulon near Ogden, Utah during muzzle loading season in 1993. It was my first trip that took me into the Rocky Mountains, and up to ten thousand feet. The terrain we were hunting was generally steep and covered with brush or small trees. Did I mention that it was steep? That trip taught me a lot about hunting the Rocky Mountains. That first day out we covered a lot of territory, generally staying high and glassing the valleys and bowls. The conditions were very dry, so walking quietly was almost impossible. We saw a few deer but they weren't very cooperative. The previous winter had been a bad one, and the deer herd was down. The first valley we glassed held thirty bucks the previous year, and we glassed only one two and a half year old. The remainder of the hunt found bucks, but not very many of them and all of the same age class.

So what did I learn during that hunt? I learned things like I had no clue how to estimate ranges in the mountains and I didn't like hunting anything except grouse with open sights. I also learned not to buy something brand new and take it along without a back up. No, not boots, they were well broken in. I had purchased a very expensive set of gortex thinsulate gloves and those were the only pair that I had brought. The problem? My hands would sweat going up the first hill and then freeze from being cold and wet for the rest of the day. I never could get those gloves dry, and I ended up giving them away.

Big country like this requires a hunter to be in shape to maximize the chances for success.

Something else I learned was how wonderful duct tape is. At that time I really didn't know about wearing a fairly tight thin sock beneath an insulating sock. This allows the movement of the outer sock against the inner sock rather than your foot. I did wear two socks, but by the second day I had developed a few blisters. The other hunter in camp asked if I had any duct tape, and I replied that I did. He told me to put it over the blister and it would protect it.

That worked like a charm, and it's something I've used through the years on more than one occasion.

The point that I really took away from that hunt was that I loved being in the mountains. I also learned that spot and stalk hunting was a lot of fun, and I had to find a way to do that again. I have spent many falls in the mountains since, and have used the lessons learned on that hunt.

Perhaps the biggest lesson I returned home with is that there's no such thing as being in too good shape physically when you're headed to the mountains. Rulon related an experience where a hunter got out of his truck, walked about thirty yards and ended up right back in the truck. His hunt was over, he simply couldn't deal with the elevation or the steepness of the mountains. My guess is that he had no clue what he was getting himself into, did not get into any kind of shape and he walked the same thirty yards I did. It's almost impossible to describe to a flatlander what it's really like to hunt the Rocky Mountains at elevation. In most places, there's simply nothing to compare it to. There are unnamed hills in the Rockies that are taller and steeper than some our most notable mountains in the Adirondack's of northern New York.

I wouldn't even think about a hunt in the Rockies or any other significant mountain range without getting in shape. My exercise routines have changed through the years, but the one thing that hasn't changed is that they require time and hard work. When I was younger and my knees didn't mind the pounding like they do now, I'd jog some logging trails by my office during the week and then head for Ampersand Mountain up in the Adirondacks on one day during the weekend. As the years passed I switched to mountain bikes and that worked pretty well, except that the muscles used for climbing are slightly different than those used for biking. I've settled on walking up and down steep hills with weight on my back. As my hunts approach, I still like to head for Ampersand on the weekends. It's a two hour drive, but the mountain is perfect for training. The trail starts out fairly flat, for a good warm up and then turns very steep, simulating some of the mountains I tackle out west. It's about a five mile round trip and the elevation change is about eighteen hundred feet. Depending on how much weight I've got on my back, and how my knees feel on the trip down the round trip generally ranges between two and a half and three hours. The one thing it can't simulate is the lack of oxygen. I think the only way to do that would be to hike up the mountain with a plastic bag over your head. Although more oxygen would probably still get through than you find at ten thousand feet.

One year after painfully getting in shape I was in Idaho hunting solo for mule deer. I had spent a couple of days in the low lands crunching through the crusty snow and found not so much as a single track. On the other hand, there were plenty of human tracks. On the third morning it was crystal clear and about five degrees, and I was exploring a new area. All of a sudden a bugle pierced the dawn. The bugle had come from the tallest mountain that I could see. I figured if he was high, the mule deer might be up there as well. The mountain was very steep, very tall and intimidating, but I really felt like it was the only option I had. I stripped down and started up the slope. Much to my surprise, by taking it easy I steadily progressed up the mountain and was at the top in about an hour and a half. The deer and elk were up there, and the other hunters weren't. I didn't take a monster buck up there but by being in shape and out walking the other guys I gave myself every opportunity for success.

Chapter 11
Frozen Hands Buck
1994 & 1996

I raced along the top of the ridge paralleling the buck bowling his way through the thick cover of the swamp as well as I could. I quickly fell behind, but noticed that he was starting to turn up the hill in front of me.

I was up in Saskatchewan hunting with Silver Tip Outfitters again. This time with my father along and a muzzle loader in hand. My father's deer hunting experience was pretty typical of a New Yorker. He saw many more does than bucks and would take the occasional year and a half old buck. Being a teacher, he couldn't really break away to go on any trips with me, until he retired. Then it was time for me to strike. I managed to talk him into a trip to Saskatchewan for whitetails.

The problem with Saskatchewan in November was some pretty extreme temperatures, so I suggested a muzzle loader hunt earlier in the fall. With some help from his friends and other members of the family, we bought him a Knight muzzle loader for his retirement. I decided to head back to Silver Tip Outfitters again. The DeBiennes are great people who I enjoyed spending time with and I knew my father would too. Having taken three good bucks with Garry and seeing some other big boys had me thinking that it was the perfect place to take my father. We spent the summer shooting and getting our loads nailed down.

Pretty soon we were on our way. I was surprised to see that they actually grew grass in Saskatchewan and it wasn't white, it was in fact green. There were even leaves still on the trees and there wasn't any ice anywhere. We got settled in to our cabin and went over to Garry and Zay's. Introductions were made and we got caught up. We decided to make sure our rifles were still zeroed so we got set up on a picnic table and took a few shots. Garry was intrigued with the guns and decided to fire one. The only problem was that he got a little close to the scope (or visa versa) and pretty soon there was a blood trail. Since other people's pain is always a good source for amusement, we all got a good laugh from the scope tracks. Well, at least two out of three of us did. We spent an enjoyable evening chatting with the family, and then headed off to the sack.

 The next morning bright and early we piled into my truck and headed to Garry's where we piled into his truck and started the drive around the lake. An hour later, my father and I were dropped off in our stands, full of anticipation. The only thing that bothered me was that the temperatures were very warm. Good for dad, bad for deer. I spent the whole day on the stand and ended up seeing two year and a half old bucks, one sporting nine points and a few flatheads. My father didn't fair much better. The next few days were the same, with very few deer sightings. At some point, Garry broke out his fishing boat and we ended up boating across the lake to a few of the stands in fifteen minutes rather than driving all the way around in an hour. One day, we were standing around in bright sunshine and shirtsleeves discussing what we should do. Garry suggested getting some fishing licenses and going after some walleyes. While I like fishing, I knew the size of the bucks that were running around the area, so there was no temptation for me. My father on the other hand is a hard core fisherman and I thought he'd go for it, but he resisted.

 It was very obvious to me that no matter what we did, the overwhelming majority of the deer movement was happening at night, it was simply too warm during the day. Part of Garry's hunting area was right on the border of where nonresidents could hunt. There was a large field on the border, and I wondered if the deer were feeding in the field all night and if they came back across the border into the woods late enough in the morning to catch them. We decided to give it a shot, so the next morning we started down the border. My father was taking his time getting ready, so I walked a hundred yards down the line. I heard grunting behind me and saw him walking toward me, therefore making the assumption that he was doing the calling. Unfortunately, what was happening is that Garry saw two good bucks doing just what we thought they'd do and was trying to get my father's attention. They walked right by Garry within easy shooting distance.

 We ran into a few more deer sneaking through, but no shooters. We tried catching them coming out of the woods into the field in the evening, but they were coming out too late. We also tried getting on stand deeper in the woods in the morning well before sunrise, but it didn't work. We were busted in that area. My father did have a herd of elk walk right by him and it was amusing to hear him describe the big bull looking down on him behind the downfall and wondering whether he should be worried.

We went to a different area that had trails running deep into the bush. Garry set dad up on a stand overlooking a big bowl with heavy cover all around and we continued on, still hunting the heavy cover. We walked a few miles in and I found a good place to sit and watch a likely looking ridge line. Garry retreated to the main road. I ended up seeing a doe, and that was it.

The light was fading fast and I decided to still hunt back to my father, pick him up at sunset and meet Garry. I was slowly working my way along the trail, and had traveled almost all the way back. I was at the top of a hill, with the trail dropping down into the bowl where my father was. I had timed it well, and started down the hill. After two steps the brush exploded sixty yards in front of me. I caught a glimpse of a huge buck crashing into the swamp. My guess from that one look was that he was something in the one sixty class. As described earlier, I took off at a sprint to parallel him.

When he turned up the hill, I dropped to one knee and clicked off the safety. I was a split second slow getting on him and he stopped in some brush with just his rear end showing at about a hundred yards. He stood like that for a few minutes, probably looking back to see if I was pursuing him. Then he took a few steps forward and I never saw him again. I moved forward and kept trying to pick him out in the brush, but he was gone. I knew right then that under the circumstances, that was my one and only opportunity for the trip.

This was exactly the type of buck I wanted my father to see, and he should have been close by, so I hurried back to the designated meeting place. After talking for a few moments, it seemed that my father had left his stand just a few minutes before the buck showed up.

We discussed what to do that evening and decided to head back into the thick bush where I had taken my first Canadian whitetail. I went all the way in to where I had shot the buck and hardly recognized the area it was so grown up. I spent the day in there and only saw a doe. My father didn't fare much better, but Garry saw a nice buck, again being just a little too far away from dad to get his attention. The rest of the hunt passed with the same general outcome, the big bucks simply were not moving during daylight hours, and bedding in heavy cover.

Following our muzzle loader hunt in Saskatchewan and not showing my father a big buck, I really wanted him to experience seeing some mature animals. The problem is that he's not wild about temperatures approaching absolute zero. Knowing that his chances of seeing a good buck increased dramatically during the rut, I relentlessly bugged him about it until he finally gave in. If nothing else, I knew that he and Garry would have a good time sitting in the truck swapping stories. Of course I may have downplayed the temperatures a little bit, but I figured they had good hospitals in Saskatoon and they're doing great things with skin grafts these days.

We again made the drive north, with rifles in hand and another hundred pounds of clothing. We arrived at Garry and Zay's house and were just getting settled in when there was some commotion downstairs. A beautiful one sixty class ten point was walking past the house in the woods. Unfortunately, we were in the resident only area and could only watch the buck as he moved off in search of does. A little while later, a smaller ten point decided to start feeding at the bird feeder right by the house. It was a painful time.

Knowing that my father might have some trouble with the temperatures, Garry had made a fully enclosed blind and had dug it into a hillside. So my father would be headed there, and I'd be headed to another stand where I had had some success previously. The morning came, and I could hear the exclamation when dad stepped out of the door. He's lived a good portion of his life in upstate New York, and cold temperatures are pretty normal during the winter, but going hunting at twenty below zero is a whole lot different than walking out of a store and getting in your car at twenty below zero. We drove the familiar route around the lake since Garry refused to cut a path for the boat or drive across the ice and pretty soon we were ready to drop my father off. My last piece of advice before he stepped out of the truck was, "Don't freeze your hands." In the ten minutes it took to get to the blind, of course he froze his hands, and it took a good amount of time with the heat packs and the hand muff to get them to work again. My father likes to take a soda with him on stand, and shortly after sunrise he noticed that the soda was freezing. He figured he'd set it on the edge of the blind in the sun and it should be all right. He sat there and watched it freeze solid in the next few minutes. Welcome to Saskatchewan dad.

I saw a few bucks, but nothing close to a shooter. My father saw a few bucks as well, so things were looking up. A stand switch in the morning brought a wolf sighting to my father. That's one of those neat things that happen when you're out in the bush. When he first saw it, he was initially wondering what the heck a dog was doing out there. So the day ended with a unique experience for dad but again no shooters for either of us. On the third day, dad was back in the bunker, the affectionate name for the blind. He saw a huge bodied buck headed down the hill. I think by that time, he would have shot just about anything to get back into the truck, but he said the buck looked big to him so he squeezed the trigger. As I came out to the road at the end of the day, I was told the news. It might have been more satisfying for me than my father. I think he was just happy to get in out of the cold. I looked at the buck, and he reminded me of the first buck I took in Saskatchewan. Huge shoulders, tapering down to a skinny rear end, with very little fat from running during the rut. It's amazing that any of these bucks manage to make it through those harsh winters after running themselves ragged. Back at Garry's place, we weighed the dressed buck, and the scale touched two hundred pounds on the button.

Author's father, Stan Bingham with a big bodied Canadian whitetail. This was his first and last trip to Saskatchewan in November for some reason.

The next few days for me was just one long cold day on the stand after another. We finally made it to Sunday, which meant sleeping in and no hunting allowed. It also meant seeing cruising bucks walking past the house that left me shaking my head. I think we ended up seeing a half dozen very nice bucks sauntering past the windows.

Then it was back into the stand for me, with more of the same. I was seeing deer, but no bucks with any age. On day nine of the hunt, I was in a tree stand and I sensed something behind me, close. I slowly turned and saw brown coming through the trees. The buck slowly walked directly under my stand, allowing me to get a good look. Nine days of sitting in frigid tree stands took their toll. Frankly I was just worn out, and I decided that the eight pointer would fill the bill. He dropped at the shot, and more importantly, wasn't as big as dad's. We left Garry and Zay the following day after a very enjoyable couple of weeks.

Chapter 12
Alaskan Adventure
1995

I'd been crawling through two foot high wet grass and sloshing down a creek bed in the "hunker" position for the better part of an hour. I belly crawled up a small rise and pushed the soaked grass apart with my Browning Stainless Stalker. I spotted the bedded bull right where I had left him three hundred yards ago. I was wet, sweating, my scope was fogged, my glasses were steamed and I was having the time of my life. I was somewhere just east of the middle of nowhere, which put me in southwestern Alaska.

My trip began about the time that I got my notification from the Wyoming Game Department in late February that the elk with my name on it would get another year to grow before I could get a crack at him. I quickly decided to try and move up the timeline on the Alaska trip that I had planned for the following year. Lacking the research time required to properly plan a hunt such as this, I turned to Cabelas Outdoor Adventures. It seems like every piece of sporting equipment that I own came from Cabelas, so I knew that I could trust them to provide a quality hunt. They had an opening for a hunt beginning on the fourteenth of September, which fit into my schedule perfectly. My next task was to get a hunting partner (meat packer) to go along with me.

Jim Reape had been stationed in Fairbanks for a few years while in the Air Force. He always talked about how great it would be to get back to Alaska, but he thought that it would be too expensive. So his wife Jane and I arranged the hunt, and she got it for Jim for his birthday. She paid for the hunt, arranged his leave time with his boss, and then broke the news to him. My search for a meat packer was complete.

Following several months of planning, packing, unpacking, and packing, we found ourselves on a plane bound for Anchorage. The trip out was fairly uneventful, but long and tiring. When we finally arrived at the hotel, it didn't take us long to call it quits and turn in for the night. I woke up at about three the next morning with some pain in my lower abdomen. I figured that I had probably just strained a muscle lugging around the rocks that someone had packed for me in my duffel bag. As time went on, the pain continued to increase, and when Jim woke up at about five it was getting downright nasty. I told him that I thought we might have to take a detour before we departed, and we were soon headed for the emergency room. By the time I rolled out of the cab I was drenched in a cold sweat, and wondering if my dream trip to Alaska would consist of me seeing the airport, hotel and hospital. They hadn't even gotten around to examining me when the pain suddenly subsided, much to my relief. A few tests, and a few thousand dollars later they concluded that I had a kidney stone, and that it had probably passed through the kidney while I was at the hospital. While all of this was going on, Jim had made a few quick calls to our outfitter Lake Clark Air, and they said that they could work with us on a schedule to get us into camp that day. Given the situation, the LCA staff impressed me, and I'm grateful for their efforts. I was given a prescription for some pain medication, which I didn't fill, 'cause real men don't need pain medication ... unless of course they happen to be in pain at that moment. I was also given a few screened funnels for uh, well let's just say that they wanted to see the stone when it came out. I checked out of the hospital and told Jim to get packed because we were going hunting. He gave me a look like I had one oar in the water and my boat was taking on water. He looked at me like that all the time, so I ignored him and headed for the taxi.

Much to our astonishment given the morning's activities, we left Merrill Field at about two pm, and landed at Lake Clark about an hour later after the most spectacular flight I've ever been privileged to take. It was a rare sunny day, and we flew right through the Chigmit Mountains, passing by glaciers, dall sheep and beautiful high peaks. Unfortunately, my camera had been packed in the confusion, and I didn't get any shots. After waiting at Lake Clark for a few hours, we left in a four seat single engine plane, and headed for the middle of nowhere, near the Kuskokwim Mountains. After we got to the middle of nowhere, we were loaded into a pair of Super Cubs with balloon tires and flew into our camp just east of the middle of nowhere. During our flight into camp, I saw a bull caribou that had been taken down by wolves, and partially eaten. I wondered where my new place on the food chain was, this far from home.

As we swung around to land on a little knob that was smooth enough to serve as a runway, there were several groups of caribou within sight of the camp. I could hardly wait to get started. We lost no time in getting our tent set up, and our gear unpacked and prepared for the next day. There were four tagged out hunters there, who were scheduled to be flown out the next day. They graciously clued us in on some hot spots that they had found, one being a bend in a creek that the caribou seemed to like to funnel through. After an evening of glassing, we decided to try the bend in the creek in the morning and turned in for the night. Not to get off the subject, but imagine trying to urinate in a paper funnel at night with thirty mph winds blowing. It gets even tougher when you start laughing about it. The funnels didn't last long, sorry Doc.

After a long sleepless night, I finally started to detect a little light edging up from the east, and I crawled out of my sleeping bag. Before we left New York I had asked Jim how long the days were in Alaska this time of year. He replied that they generally lasted from sunrise to sunset. I said "Oh, just like here," and made a mental note to talk to his doctor about increasing his medication dosage for the trip. This thought flashed through my head as I stepped from the tent into the predawn gloom. A small group of caribou was visible about a quarter of a mile away, getting the morning off to a promising start. We quickly packed our day packs and headed for the stream. When we finally arrived, after walking about a mile through the tundra, Jim remarked that this would probably be as far as we would want to pack a bull out. Being a reasonable person, I whole heartily agreed that it would be plenty of work getting a caribou back to camp from our present position. We had a small hill directly in front of us, limiting our view to perhaps four hundred yards, but we could see several miles in the other directions. Several hundred caribou were visible as we settled in, with most being three to five miles off in the distance. After waiting about an hour, a caribou head suddenly materialized in front of us. We quickly scampered down to a good ambush spot and were treated to a group of about a dozen cows, calves and small bulls wandering by at about a hundred yards. Shortly thereafter, we spotted a group of about fifty animals headed slightly to the south of us, perhaps a half a mile in the distance. After a quick conference, we decided to try and head them off at the pass. We raced down the stream bed after the caribou. Well, maybe "raced" isn't quite correct, we actually stumbled, slid and scrambled. Needless to say, we didn't even get close to beating the herd to our ambush spot, and had to settle for watching them pass by at about six hundred yards. Oh well, like the song says, sometimes you're the windshield, and sometimes you're the bug. The rest of the day was fairly uneventful as we saw many caribou, but nothing close enough to get our adrenaline running. Earlier in the day, we had talked to the other hunters at the camp about our morning's activities, and they had informed us that we had stopped at the wrong stream, and the really hot crossing was further out. If we had been at the other stream, that big herd would have walked right into us.

The next morning found us walking right past the spot that was our limit for packing out a bull. I just wanted to prove that I was still young and stupid, I'm not sure what caused Jim's mental lapse. We found a good place to sit and watch, but like the previous day, the view directly in front of us was limited, due to a small rise on the other side of the creek. Once we got settled in, Jim turned to me and said that we should wait until the caribou got across the creek before we shot because it would be real tough to pack a bull across the stream. That seemed like a reasonable request, so I agreed. The morning passed quickly with just a few cows and calves slipping past us. Early in the afternoon, I decided that I heard nature calling, and headed down to the bed of the stream. All of a sudden, I heard a whistle and I immediately knew what was happening. I peeked up over the ridge and saw several caribou milling around, about a quarter mile away. I crawled back up to our vantage point and we started to glass the herd. There were several good bulls in the bunch, but it appeared that they were going to cross the stream too far away for a shot. Jim and I figured that the only way to get close to them would be to run down the stream bed. I asked him if he wanted to try it, and he gave me that one oar in the water look and said that if I saw something in there that I liked, then to go right ahead. I slid down into the water and started my stalk. Sometime during the stalk, the herd had stopped, and some of the animals had bedded. After closing the distance to about two hundred fifty yards, I set up my Harris Bipod and settled in for the shot. I found that I was just low enough that I needed to wait until the bull stood up in order to get a good shot. Luckily, the lead cow soon decided that the boys had had enough rest and started to move across in front of me. The bulls reluctantly stood and began to follow her. I waited for the animals to string out, and held slightly in front of the right shoulder to allow for the twenty or thirty mile an hour crosswind and squeezed the trigger. At the shot, the bull bucked slightly, ran a short distance towards me and then stopped. I racked another shell into the chamber, and then for some reason I lost track of which caribou was mine. They were all just standing there looking at me. I was just beginning to panic when one of the animals started to stagger. A few seconds later the bull went down and it was all over. As I walked up to the bull, he kept getting bigger and bigger until I was sure that I had a moose lying on the ground. Jim caught up to me shortly thereafter, he was muttering something about being on the wrong side of the stream and I'm pretty sure he was insulting my ancestry. I figured he was just testy because he had missed his nap. We quartered the bull, and I loaded a front shoulder on Jim, pointed the way back to the camp and sent him on his way. At some point, Jim had exhausted his list of ancestral insults and had switched to suggesting things that were anatomically impossible. He was still coming up with some very inventive remarks as he wandered off over the tundra out of hearing range. I removed the antlers from the head, and stashed them down by the creek. Then I loaded my day pack, a front shoulder and the game bag with the miscellaneous cuts of meat on my frame and staggered off towards camp, once again proving beyond a shadow of a doubt that I was still young and stupid. The day was about shot, so we decided to return the next day for the rest of the meat and the antlers.

Some severe wind and rain began at about midnight that night, and lasted right through the next day, essentially keeping us pinned in camp. The following day brought heavy winds, but the downpour had subsided. We threw on our pack frames and headed out to retrieve the remainder of the bull. We had just rounded the corner of the hill about two hundred yards from camp, when I spotted a group of fifty caribou about a half a mile away moving towards us. I turned to Jim and asked him if he wanted to shoot a caribou. Without waiting for an answer, I ran to a small group of bushes about a hundred yards in front of us. I quickly glassed the group and found at least two bulls that looked good. I had brought along my rifle for bear protection, but Jim had left his back at camp. So Jim familiarized himself with my rifle as I continued to glass the herd, which was making a beeline right for us. As the herd got into range, Jim knelt down on the edge of the bush and aimed at a big bull about seventy yards away. He touched off the 300 Win Mag and the bull dropped in his tracks. We walked over to the bull, and after the usual backslapping and congratulations, decided to go get the rest of my bull before taking care of Jim's bull.

A few hours later, we arrived back at camp with the last of my caribou, and had found that the intense wind had pulled a few stakes on our tent. We spent a few moments reinforcing the structure with extra stakes, and returned to Jim's bull to begin packing it back to camp. As we topped the rise with our first load of meat it became apparent that our tent had taken on the unique shape of a pancake. Let me tell you, when you're two hundred fifty miles into the wilderness, that is not the most welcome sight in the world. We examined the tent and found that a few of the pole ferrules had broken with the constant pounding of the wind, which had reached a velocity that made it difficult to even stand up, on top of the ridge. To make matters worse, not only did the tent collapse, but it had also ripped. We decided to set up camp in the vestibule, which would have worked out great, except for the rip that suddenly appeared along the doorway.

We took down the now useless vestibule and quickly placed an orange flag on the ground for our bush pilots, indicating that we had some trouble, and it sure would be nice of them to drop in for a visit. I really didn't expect to see anyone flying in that weather, as they'd probably have to land going backwards.

"Meat packer" Jim Reape with his nice bull, taken with the author's rifle.

We packed up all of our nonessential gear in garbage bags, and used our cots and other equipment to prop up the tent enough so that we could lie on the ground between the cots. Then we retrieved the rest of Jim's caribou, and I complained bitterly about the full three hundred yards that I had to pack his bull, but he wasn't really all that compassionate about my discomfort. Except for a few showers and the constant high wind, the night passed fairly uneventfully, and we looked forward to getting into a plane the next day.

Somewhere around mid morning one of our pilots who was on a meat run landed, and we told him about our situation. He said that he would try to get back in to pick us up that evening. He also said that he might not be able to make it back, and asked if we could make it through another night. We told him that we could if we needed to. If I had known the kind of night that we were in for, I would have tied myself to the wing strut right there and then. We waved to the pilot as he took off and spent the rest of the day camera hunting, napping, and reading.

That night the wind picked up to an unbelievable level. It was so windy there were even white caps in the water jug. As I laid there on the two hundred and thirty seven rocks (I counted them) that made up my bed, I went through some emergency procedures we could use if the tent went bye bye. The nearest real cover was miles away, but we did have a tarp covering our food cache that we could secure with rocks and huddle under. I was just wondering how much of our clothes and equipment we would be able to find in the morning when I heard two loud cracks, and the weight of the tent falling on my face. A few more poles had given way, and the wind was pressing the tent fabric down on us with quite a bit of force. The good news was that we still had a tent that was offering some protection from the elements. My pulse had just gotten down to a restful hundred and fifty beats per minute when I heard Jim say, "Hey Glenn I need a flashlight, I don't think we've got a fly." I quickly turned on the light, and we made a survey of the situation, determining that we did still have a fly, it just wasn't very high above us or in one piece. We spent the rest of the night with the tent bouncing against our faces, but without any further incidents.

In the morning we made more repairs to the tent, but it was clear that it was not going to last much longer. We spent the day bursting out of the tent every time we heard something that remotely resembled a motor, and we did some more camera hunting. By late afternoon, it was clear that we were in for another night in the bush. Compared with the previous night, the night was a breeze and we anxiously awaited dawn and the sound of bush planes.

The "pancake" tent, all propped up and ready for more of the typhoon.

The next morning, the wind was down to perhaps thirty mph, but it began to rain quite heavily, and we spent the morning watching our pancake tent turn into a swimming pool. We were just making a gourmet lunch of peanut butter and jelly sandwiches, when we heard the sound of a plane. Jim jumped out of the tent and waved to the plane, which was circling around for a landing. We ran up to the plane, and told our pilot that our tent was becoming a swamp. He told us to get packed up, and we'd leave right then. We quickly tore down the tent as our second plane landed. We got packed and were in the air within a half hour. The ride back to Lake Clark was extremely bumpy, and Jim got to test out how waterproof his hat was the hard way. I'll let you use your imagination for just how he did that.

As we headed back to Anchorage, I reflected back on the past week's events. We probably saw five thousand caribou, and got to experience the raw power and beauty that is the essence of Alaska. I promised myself that I would find a way to make a return trip.

Chapter 13
Newfoundland Aye Bye
1998

I drove up to Montreal from my upstate New York home, the border crossing had been a no hassle one, as usual. In fact the trip was a no hassle one, until I got close to Montreal and hit the traffic. I was headed for a hotel to spend the night, and managed to hit the city at what was apparently rush hour. I managed to head in the right direction, and at one point I could actually see my hotel no more than a hundred yards away. The only problem was the concrete barricade between us and an endless sea of one way streets. I drove around for a while, and managed to actually see the hotel a second time, still sitting there, mocking me. Feeling like a rat in a maze and driving around for the better part of an hour I finally found the combination to get me over there and gratefully pulled in to the hotel parking lot.

When I made my reservation I had been told that they would allow my truck to be parked there during the duration of my hunt, while I took the shuttle to the airport in the morning. Luckily I had decided to confirm this while I was getting checked in, and found that the planets were no longer aligned properly for that little plan to succeed. I would not be allowed to leave my truck, and there was no shuttle to the airport. If I had not wanted to face that traffic again, I probably would have found another hotel, but I swallowed my tongue, thanked the nice lady and went to my room to try and figure out where the airport was.

I survived the trip to the airport, and it was with great relief that I sank into my seat bound for Newfoundland. The flight was relatively short, and my impression upon landing in Deer Lake was a vast land of brush, evergreens and water. I took a cab to the hotel and got checked in. Soon there was a knock on my door and Moose Valley outfitter Dean MacDonald introduced himself. Dean seemed like a nice guy, and we chatted as we got the license paperwork taken care of. He mentioned that the other hunter was from upstate New York as well. Soon I was introduced to Steve Sinclair. I recognized him immediately, but couldn't place where I knew him from. He asked where I was from and I answered "Great Bend." He said, "Indiana?" I responded that I thought he was from somewhere around my home of Great Bend, NY. It turned out that he owned a restaurant about ten miles down the road from my house. It's a small world out there.

After a bit of a wait the next morning, we were loaded on the floatplane for the trip into camp. We flew over mostly brushy terrain interspersed with spruce forests and some open grasslands. There were an endless supply of ponds, swamps and lakes scattered in between the tall hillsides. Shortly the plane started to descend, and circled into a large lake, where we were treated to a smooth landing. We taxied up to a dock, and we were introduced to the rest of the team as we unloaded the plane. We took our luggage into the brand new cabin that they had spent the summer constructing, complete with running water.

We got settled in, got unpacked and prepared for the next morning. Since we had some time, I took a walk up the hill behind camp. It was a pretty good climb, but it was worth the effort when I topped out into a relatively open area with a great view of the surrounding land. I could see several small groups of caribou scattered a few miles away, and as I topped one small hill, there was a black bear feeding about four hundred yards away. It was just the kind of setting that I love, and had me primed for the hunt. I returned to camp and found an excellent meal waiting.

As we ate, we talked about our jobs and our lives. Dean asked Steve what kind of restaurant he had. He said something about it not being a fast food restaurant. Never one to miss an opening, I quickly confirmed that by telling everyone it was very slow. Some people laughed more than others ...

One thing that struck me as being very unique was the Newfoundland accent. I had never heard an accent quite like it, and it took me a little while to catch on. One of the guides turned to me and said, "Whataya shoot'n dair bye?" I was pretty sure that I got the "What are you shooting?" part, but the "dair bye" had me a little confused. I answered that I was shooting a three hundred Win Mag, and apparently that was the right answer, because I got an "Okay, dair's da weapon, aye." After a while I got my brain around the "dair" is "there", "da" is "the", "wit" is "with", "bye" is "boy", etc. I found that I could have fallen into their speech patterns very easily and probably could have been mistaken for a native inside a month. The evening passed quickly and soon it was time to turn in and try to get some sleep.

The next morning Dean and I jumped into the boat and motored across the lake for about two miles where we tied it to shore. I hadn't seen any minnows anywhere and asked about the fishing. Dean told me that none of the lakes up where we were held any fish at all. It was very hard to believe, but the only kind of fishing that could be done up there were for leaches. We struggled up through the willow thickets and found some open area as we went up the hill. We worked our way from high spot to high spot glassing as we went. The weather was clear and cool, a perfect day for spot and stalk hunting. We saw a few cows scattered in the thick brush as we continued to work higher into the terrain.

We found one open area bordered by thick brush that transitioned into thick trees. As we glassed the brush, a flash of yellow suddenly reflected in the sunlight. We saw a large set of paddles above the brush. The bull cleared briefly, and we could tell he was a good one. Dean asked me if I could hit him from our current position. Lacking a range finder, the bull looked like he was a long ways away and I didn't feel comfortable with the shot. We started to work our way toward the bull, using the brush for cover. As we got closer to where we thought he should be, we stopped and scanned the bush. We didn't see a thing. Finally, Dean indicated a hill behind us and suggested that we climb it to see if we could locate the bull. We were about half way up, when we spotted him in the brush and scrambled down the hill toward him. Soon I could see the bull clearly and guessed that he was inside two hundred yards. I grabbed Dean's pack and silently showed him that we were close enough and I was ready to take a shot.

My bipod was already extended as I settled into a sitting position and got the crosshairs to settle on the bulls shoulder. I squeezed the trigger and sent the Nosler partition down range. The bull barely reacted to the shot and only moved off a short ways. We ran to the side and I tried an off hand shot at the bull. The bull moved into the bush some more and we lost sight of him. Dean turned to me and asked if I had hit him. I told him that I thought I had made a good shot.

We slowly eased up to the last spot that we saw him and found a few splashes of blood. Dean climbed a tree to see if he could see the bull, and quickly signaled that he was down, just thirty yards ahead. As we approached the bull he just kept growing and growing. We checked to make sure he was done, and I stood there in awe of the size of the animal. He was absolutely huge.

Author with a big Newfoundland moose.

After taking some pictures we started to quarter him. As I dragged a hind leg away, it occurred to me that it was almost like dragging a full grown whitetail. We got him quartered and into the game bags. Dean marked a tree for the return trip and we headed out with the cape and antlers. How on earth a bull moose can walk through those willow thickets, I have no idea. I got so frustrated with those antlers I almost left them behind a few times. We did finally break into the open and found our boat right where we left it, a very welcome sight. One bull down, one to go.

I spent the next day accompanying Steve and found out that the hills aren't quite as steep without a gun on your back. We saw a few animals, but no good bulls presented a shot. The next few days I spent walking around, glassing and taking pictures. I saw all kinds of great country and Steve ended up taking a nice bull as well. I was soon on the way home with a nice rack and a few boxes of excellent moose meat. The trip would have ended perfectly if I hadn't gotten lost in Montreal on the way home.

Chapter 14
Mule Deer Education
1997–2001

My first hunt for mule deer in Utah wasn't successful. But I did learn a lot about hunting them. My next bit of education came courtesy of Golden Gate Outfitters in 1997.

I drove to the outskirts of Denver following a bow hunt in Wisconsin during which I tried several different pieces of public land. While I saw several bucks, they were all youngsters, so I let them go. One interesting event did occur while I was there however, a snowstorm came through and dropped several inches of heavy wet snow on the ground. What was more interesting was that the same storm had gone through Denver and had dropped a few feet of snow. Anxious to see the area and concerned about running into bad road conditions along the way, I departed Wisconsin a day early and headed for Colorado. The trip was uneventful, so I arrived early and spent a day wandering around the countryside. Ironically, I drove past some of the same ground I'd be hunting later on.

I met guide Mike Smith at a designated location and he led me up the long steep trail to a beautiful lodge located on a high peak. I met owner Randy Christensen, his wife Holly and his son Marty at the lodge and got settled in my room. The property Randy has for his mule deer hunting is just west of Denver and varies from steep rugged terrain to rolling hills. The elevation varies from about seven to eight thousand feet, which to a flatlander is high. It is generally a mix of scrub brush and timber, with some open grasslands thrown in as well. Depending on the snow depths in the higher country, elk can be seen on the ranch as well as they migrate down to better forage. It was just that kind of year, and a spotting scope was set up on the kitchen table focused on the elk a couple of miles away on a hill side. Several of the hunters who were coming into camp had elk tags so they were a welcome sight.

I met guide Art Warren and the other hunters in camp, and we headed for the range to make sure the rifles were still on. After that Art took me around and showed me some of the ranch. Right at sunset we glassed several deer on a hill about a half mile away, including a few good bucks. We decided to return to the spot in the morning to see if they were still there. After a sleepless night and a good breakfast we headed out before daybreak. After some glassing, we located the group still in the same basic location. Art pointed out the route we'd have to walk to get to them and while it looked intimidating, I was too excited about the opportunity to take my first mule deer to be very concerned.

We started trudging up and down hills keeping the wind in our favor. We finally reached the large hill that would serve as our final bit of cover. We slowed our ascent and I caught my breath as we crept through the sparse cover. Soon we could see the slope where the herd had been located. The entire stalk had taken about an hour, so we weren't sure exactly where they were. Art suddenly spotted movement so we froze and studied the area. The movement soon became a buck with very light colored antlers. To a whitetail hunter from the east he looked huge to me. He was a typical four point with antlers that tipped outward. We whispered back and forth about taking the buck, and I finally decided to see if I could get a shot.

I dropped the legs on my bipod and tried to get into a sitting position on the slope. I finally settled on sort of a compromise with one leg of the bipod on the ground and using a tree as a second point to anchor the gun. The buck was just under two hundred yards, and I soon had the crosshairs bouncing on his rib cage. A few deep breaths steadied me enough so that I was able to squeeze the trigger. At the shot, the buck turn and started running away dragging a leg. Art said, "Hit him again, you shot him in the leg!" I frantically worked another round into the chamber swearing under my breath. I was just getting back on the buck when he started to sag, and soon he was down. I kept the gun on him just to make sure, but he was done.

We walked up to the buck, and I was thrilled with my first mule deer. As the week progressed, four bull elk and four very nice mule deer found their way to the skinning pole including one buck that exceeded thirty inches. I spent some time on the ranch glassing and taking pictures and knew that I'd be back.

So, two years later I was right back in the same spot anxious to see what kind of deer I would see. After getting caught up with Randy we talked about the hunt. Randy said that Marty would be my guide.

Author with his first mule deer, setting the stage for some great adventures through the years.

The morning dawned a dreary foggy mess with some snow thrown in for good measure. At times the visibility was down under a hundred yards. We glassed when we could and even took a little walk around a basin, but the conditions were making it very difficult to hunt. The afternoon was filled with more of the same until right before sunset when the fog lifted a little. We stopped at a favorite glassing location and spotted several deer about a half mile away. One of them looked like a very good buck, but there was still enough fog present that we weren't really sure. We decided to make a stalk and see what he looked like from a better vantage point.

As I started up the hill, I quickly became overheated and my glasses fogged up. Between my glasses being fogged, the foggy air, and the snow on the ground the world was just a white haze to me. Every time I'd try to smear the fog off my glasses, they'd just fog up in a few seconds, so I quit trying. As a result, I was in my own little foggy world of white, trying to follow the dark blob that I assumed was Marty. Since I couldn't see, I would very often stumble and slip as I worked my way up the slope.

Marty, being the nice kid that he was, decided that apparently I had no idea how to walk up a hill, and tried to tell me how to position my feet on the slope to stop slipping. What he didn't realize is that I just plain couldn't see my feet, the ground.... anything. If I could have caught my breath, I would have told him so, but I just agreed and we headed up again. To this day I laugh every time I think about this poor kid trying to teach me how to walk up a hill.

Finally we reached the top of the hill and I crawled into a prone position with the bipod down. I'd smear my glasses and get about five seconds to look for the buck before they'd fog up again. Marty and I talked back and forth about where the buck was, using different trees as reference points. Eventually we got it straightened out and I got a good look at the buck. From just under three hundred yards he looked very good to me. He wasn't very wide, but he was tall with good mass and deep forks. I settled into the snow, smeared my glasses one more time, centered the crosshairs on the shoulder end of the blob and squeezed the trigger. I lost sight of the buck, but we soon saw him bedded with his head up. A follow up shot later and the buck was mine. I stumbled up another hill and was soon looking at a very nice blob, as darkness settled around us.

Width isn't everything. Mass and deep forks made this buck a keeper.

Once again I spent the remainder of the hunt wandering the ranch, helping with spotting duties and taking more pictures. That ranch was like a haven to me, and I enjoyed every second I spent there. I booked with Randy before I left for 2001 and headed back down the road to New York.

The two years passed quickly as they seem to do and I found myself crawling back up the steep road to the lodge. Art dropped by in the afternoon and we headed out to see what we could find. We hadn't gone far when I glimpsed some movement about fifty yards away in the bottom of a small drainage. It somehow didn't look like a deer, but I wasn't sure what I had seen. We glassed the area for a few moments and then started on our way. I looked back over my shoulder one last time and couldn't believe my eyes. An extra large mountain lion was laying on a rock watching us. We watched the big cat for a while, marveling at the basketball sized head, and then continued on our way.

An interesting side note is that a few days later one of the other guides saw some magpies in the area, and found the carcass of a young buck in the gully. A group of us went down to investigate and found that the deer had been claimed by a skunk. It's amazing how one little charging skunk can make a group of grown men scatter like a herd of zebra being attacked by a lion.

The top picture shows the skunk guarding his deer carcass, the bottom picture shows why good glasses are imperative in big country.

After getting settled in to the familiar surroundings, we started talking about the next morning's hunt. Mike Smith had drawn the short straw, and was forced to guide me. Fortunately for him I was paired up with another hunter, and I drew my own short straw, so it was his first shot. The first morning we drove down into a deep steep gulch. At least I think it's steep, it's hard to tell with your eyes closed. We parked at one end, with arrangements to be picked up at the other end.

Once we reached the first ridgeline, Mike told me that they'd take a lower route down the gully and I could walk the high route. He explained where we'd meet our ride, (Marty) which was about two hours away. I thoroughly enjoyed myself, hitting a high spot and glassing for a while, then moving on to the next. I saw a few deer, but nothing to get my blood boiling. They had the same luck, but it was a great start to the hunt so I didn't really care.

We headed back and met with one of the other guides, who said that they had spotted a good buck that one of the other hunters had passed up, looking for Godzilla. We crept into the area and glassed, then we moved forward and glassed some more. We continued this until Mike spotted the buck bedded under a juniper. They felt like they needed to get closer, so they eased up while I remained in place. A shot later, and a nice buck was lying on the hillside. After the congratulations and picture taking we took him back to the skinning pole. Once that was done, it was my turn on the trigger. The afternoon turned up one monster buck late in the afternoon in an area that we could not get to in time, so we headed back to the lodge.

The next morning, Mike wanted to try looking at a section of the ranch he had not walked before. After making arrangements with Marty for another pickup we started off in the early morning light. We saw a few deer, but nothing very big. The highlight of the morning was spooking a bighorn sheep off a ridgeline we were walking. We made it to our designated pickup point and after waiting a while we heard Marty coming down the trail. He told us that he had seen a big buck on the way down to pick us up, so we were soon on our way to see if we could find him. We parked in the general area Marty had seen the buck and started walking up the gully. Suddenly, there he was, running above us a few hundred yards away. All I could see was serious mass on the antlers and a huge body. I swung on the buck, but couldn't catch up to him before he disappeared. I got up and ran trying to parallel the buck, but never saw him again. We drove further down to see if we could see him, but he had vanished. We decided to head back and started up the hill. All of a sudden there was a buck on the hillside well out in front of us. I have no idea how he covered the amount of ground that he did so quickly. He had slowed to a walk, and I ranged him at two hundred sixty five yards. I dropped the bipod and settled into a prone position just about the same time the buck stopped. Mike could see that he was a 3x3 and asked if I still wanted to take him. I answered by clicking the safety off. He also told me that we could get closer if we needed to, but I told him I was okay. I drifted the crosshairs just a bit low on his chest and squeezed the trigger. The buck immediately collapsed and started to tumble down the hill, then was still.

We climbed up to take a look at the buck, and I was ecstatic to find just how much mass the buck carried. He was a big mature three by three, with huge bases, and the mass carrying up through the rest of the antler. Mike said that it was a buck that he had seen in velvet, and had actually snapped a few pictures. That buck carries the most mass of any buck that I've seen before or since. Another successful hunt wrapped up with the Golden Gate crew.

One aspect of my mule deer education actually started on a whitetail hunt in Idaho. The buck was probably very close to eight hundred yards away, and I could see flies buzzing around his head. I was looking through my guide's Leica spotting scope. About all I could do with my spotting scope was to determine that it was a buck. I had gotten what I believed was a heck of a bargain on what I thought was a fairly well known manufacturer. It might has well have been a child's toy when I compared it to the Leica.

Later that same year, Randy Christensen handed me a pair of Swarovski ten by fifty binoculars, remarking that his wife had gotten him a birthday present, and a Christmas present, and next year's birthday present, and maybe the following one as well.

I had invested a lot of money in what I thought were a very good pair of binoculars. Definitely a step up from the cheapo's. After looking through the Swarovski's however, I felt like running over my binoculars with my truck. There was absolutely no comparison. I could not believe the difference, and it wasn't even low light conditions. That evening, after looking through his binoculars, I was even more impressed, it was like someone turned on a light.

My uninformed opinion is that the top makers in this arena are probably all more or less the same. Like everything else, everyone has their favorites for one reason or another; I just know that all the top end glass tends to look very good to my eye. Is the top end glass needed for the thick northern woods? Probably not, but they can be worth their weight in gold determining whether or not an animal is worth a two mile hike up and over the top of a mountain.

After looking through Randy's glasses, I put third mortgage on my house and before the next year had passed, I was armed with a pair of Swarovski binoculars and a Leupold spotting scope. The difference in the field over the past several years has been worth every penny. I've picked up mule deer ears in the brush a few hundred yards away, and stickers on antlers a lot further away than that. I've looked at mule deer, elk and sheep on the sides of mountains over a mile away and have been able to make the decision whether they were shooters or not. Okay, I needed a little help judging the sheep, but you get the idea of what I'm talking about.

As far as I'm concerned, it's the same story with scopes. You get what you pay for. I've been a fan of the Leupold scopes for years, and have never been disappointed in their performance. The bottom line for me is to spend the most money I can afford and then a little more. This is an area where you definitely get what you pay for.

I absolutely love spot and stalk hunting. From my first hunt in the west, I thought it was the most fun way to hunt I had ever experienced. I'm a very patient person by nature, and don't mind sitting on top of a mountain and picking apart an adjacent mountain. Then, getting up and hiking to the next mountain and repeating the procedure. Over the years I've developed a glassing procedure that seems to work pretty well. As soon as I get to an area, I frantically scan the hillside for deer (substitute elk, moose, pigeons, etc) standing around in the wide open, so I can see them before my hunting partner. If that doesn't produce anything, then I somewhat less frantically scan the smaller patches of cover again looking for something obvious. If neither of these procedures produce any sightings, then what I like to do is get into a steady position, sitting or leaning against something to assure steady binoculars. Then I pick the mountain apart slowly in rows, scanning a row at the top, then working my way down the mountain row by row. If I still haven't sighted anything, I'll go back and get into the thick cover a little more, maybe focusing on a spot for a little more time than normal, looking for an antler tip or the flicking of an ear.

Good glasses are required to see three bedded bucks like this in the thick stuff. Yes, there are three.

Once I've picked my way through one spot, I get up and run to the next spot before my buddy can and repeat the procedure. Unless of course I'm at elevation, in which case I add an appropriate amount of wheezing to the equation before beginning to glass again.

A text book case of the glass quality making a difference happened in Colorado the year I upgraded my optics. After I tagged out I went to one of the standard glassing spots and started picking apart the brush a half mile away on a hillside. I caught the glint of something that quickly became an antler in heavy cover. Further dissection revealed a buck with about a twenty-seven inch spread, good forks and that classic boxy look of a great mule deer. There is no way I ever would have seen that buck with my old glasses. That one event sold me forever on the value of my new toys.

Chapter 15
Heavy Cover Whitetails
1998 & 2003

Like many people I know, I started hunting areas where I could see as much as possible. Whether it was in the woods or on the edge of a field, visibility was paramount. As time progressed, and I found shooting year and a half old bucks to be too easy and not very satisfying, I started moving into heavy cover. It seemed that the deeper I went, the more bucks I would see, and some of them even had some age to them. After almost thirty years of experimentation in New York, I've pretty much narrowed my hunting strategy down to one simple statement. For heavily hunted areas, locate the thickest, nastiest cover you can find. If there are any bucks with a few hunting seasons under their belt, that's where they'll be. An example of this happened a few years back on Fort Drum one beautiful fall day.

From my house, which at the time was right on the border of the base, it was an hour drive to get to the area. It included several varied and exciting activities such as four wheel drive rock climbing, swamp crossings, and a beaver dam ascent. It was definitely limited access for those with mental deficiencies. Luckily I'm a black belt in mental deficiencies.

Once the easy part was over, it was time to climb up a hill into my hunting area. The area I was hunting was unbelievably thick. There were places where you could fall down and never hit the ground. It took some effort to hike back in there, but the lack of hunting pressure made it worth it. I never saw a lot of deer in the area, but the chances of seeing a buck with some age were as good there as anywhere in New York, except perhaps the local zoo.

On this day I actually did something I almost never do. I sat on stand in the morning and then did some still hunting to scout a new area. I normally do almost all of my scouting during the early spring, but I had seen something interesting from the aerial photos that suggested a good funnel on a ridge that ran through some especially nasty territory. I decided to go on stand on the ground in the afternoon, and found a spot on an adjacent ridge that allowed me to see over most of the underbrush in the drainage to a few shooting lanes on the funnel.

It was within a half hour of sunset, and I was beginning to think about getting packed up and getting out when I caught some movement through the brush. An instant later a buck stepped into one of my lanes and stopped. I could see a lot of white on his head and snapped the gun to my shoulder. He caught the movement and raised his head for a better look, but it was already too late. A quick glance through the scope showed me everything I needed to see. A big mature buck with good mass and some width, a definite shooter in New York. I set the crosshairs behind his shoulder and squeezed the trigger. The buck disappeared into the brush in a flash.

The author ventured into thick cover for this New York buck.

I waited a few minutes until I couldn't stand it any more, going over the sight picture and trigger squeeze in my head. It felt right, I couldn't have missed. I walked over and started looking for some sign of a hit. After a few moments, I found some hair, and deep gouges of the buck running away. A few steps later and I could smell the distinct odor of a rutting buck. I didn't even look for blood, I just followed my nose, casting back and forth like a good bird dog. I stepped over a downfall, and he was lying there, punched through both lungs. That mixed bag of happiness, satisfaction and sadness was quickly replaced by the reality of the setting sun. I dug into my pack for my knife, and then dug some more…. and more…. "Houston, we have a problem." I muttered to myself.

   Everything came back to me in a rush. The previous night I was sitting home minding my own business and the phone rang. It was my father (no caller ID). My mother had done some deer hunting of her own with her car. Wondering why she didn't just use a gun like everyone else, I drove to the scene of the impact, greeted by the flashing lights of the state police. I figured the police were there because she failed to tag the deer, or she was using an illegal caliber headlight or something like that. They insisted however that they were there to help.

   Since they were helping, I was tasked with finding the remains of the buck. I grabbed a flashlight and started walking down the road. After a couple hundred yards I saw the tell tale glimmer of glass, then an antler lying on the pavement. The buck was a short distance away, dead. A finishing bumper was not required. "A one grill kill," I thought to myself, "Very impressive mom." I looked the buck over and he really wasn't in bad shape, so when the police asked my father if we wanted the deer he said sure. I'm told that I volunteered to take the buck and get it dressed out behind my parent's house. What I didn't volunteer for, but did anyway, was to leave my knife out in the field beside the gut pile.

   So there I was, out in the boondocks with nothing sharper than my wit, not a good prospect. "No problem, I'll just drag him out of here anyway," I thought. That thought lasted about two minutes. It was like trying to drag my sister from the mall. It was just not going to happen in that thick brush. So I headed back to the truck to see if I had anything in there to use. Of course I didn't (I do now), so I headed for the nearest phone and gave my father a call. I had him meet me somewhere with my knife and also picked up my deer carrier. I looked in the Fort Drum regulations and called the appropriate person for permission to recover the deer during hours of darkness. The person in question had never been called before with this type of request and didn't realize that they were listed in the regulations and could give permission. Several phone calls later, about an hour of wasted time, and I was on my way back to the buck.

It was very late when I pulled back in to my special parking spot. What was worse is that since I was hunting a new area, I only had reflectors marking my way in about half way. Not willing to quit yet, I grabbed the carrier, turned on my headlight and started slashing my way into the bush. After a while, I ran out of reflectors and made my way in by periodically turning off my light and getting a sense for the overall lay of the land. Then I'd confirm with my compass that I was more or less headed in the right direction. I somehow managed to walk right to him. I quickly unzipped him, got him loaded on the carrier and started dragging. A few hours later, and I was the one who was dragging. Several trips in and out of that rugged territory, combined with a very long tough drag had taken their toll. I was whipped. I still had a ways to go, so I decided to leave the buck overnight and take my chances on the coyotes. Jim Reape had volunteered to help in the morning after he went on stand for a few hours. So after a few hours sleep, I was back in the woods before sunrise. With some renewed energy I walked back in as the gray dawn started to lighten. To my relief, the coyotes had not found the deer, and in a little over an hour I had him back to the truck. I got him loaded up and started down the road. I met Jim driving out to help me, and he remarked about his perfect timing as he admired the big buck.

A few years later, another buck succumbed to this strategy. I was bow hunting an area adjacent to a heavy swamp and actually had only one real shooting lane where I could see out to about twenty-five yards. There were two major trails that intersected in front of me with a large scrape right at the intersection. It was an overcast day with a steady breeze blowing from the west. I had been sitting in my tree stand since before sunrise, and was just enjoying the mid morning when I heard a branch snap fifty yards to the west. Knowing that I'd have to act quickly for any bucks walking by, I grabbed my bow and prepared for a shot. A few seconds later, I caught movement in front of me and a nice rack buck stepped out right at the scrape. He started working the scrape and the overhanging branches as I quickly evaluated him. I could tell from the bulk of his shoulders and neck that he was a mature buck and decided to take him. I drew back and released on the broadside buck and watched the arrow disappear into the shadows.

A short tracking job later and I was standing by a nice eight point. He was four and a half years old, a true trophy in New York. I'm convinced that the only way I got him was that he felt secure enough in that heavy cover to be moving well into daylight hours. My time spent hunting in New York has waned the past several years, but when I do hit the woods, I always head for the heavy stuff. That's where the big boys live.

A small shooting lane in the heavy stuff produced this bow buck.

Chapter 16
Wyoming Double
1999

I arrived in late morning the day before my hunt was to begin after an uneventful trip. I turned off the main road and drove down the dusty dirt road, the smell of sage wafting through the truck. To my northeastern eyes, the landscape looked barren and devoid of life, and I couldn't imagine that we'd be hunting the immediate area since there must be better habitat elsewhere. How wrong I was. I pulled in, was introduced to my guide Les Snodgrass, and several other members of the staff of SNS Outfitters. I had driven to the middle of nowhere in the Thunder Basin National Grassland south of Gillette Wyoming, eager to hunt for my first pronghorn antelope and hopefully a nice mule deer.

I got settled in, grabbed a bite to eat and one of the guys asked if I wanted to try to take a pronghorn that afternoon. I was out the door and sitting in his truck before he stopped talking. We went to an adjacent ranch and began to drive around and glass. We soon found a herd with a good buck in the group, but busted them and they took off. We quickly made a wide circle and stopped just as the herd came trotting towards us. The buck was on the move and two hundred fifty yards out, so I didn't take the shot. We let them go and moved on to see what else we could find.

This particular ranch had oil wells scattered throughout the property, one of which was banging and popping like it was trying to explode. Ironically we found another group of goats right by the well, but busted them as we tried to make a stalk. The sun was quickly headed toward the horizon when we spotted another herd with a good buck. They were located in an area with some rolling hills, so a good stalk was definitely possible. We went from walking, to walking in a hunker position, to crawling on hands and knees. Soon Les spotted the buck and had me move up beside him. I had my bipod already extended and settled into a sitting position with my knee tucked up under the stock. I quickly found the goat, guessed him at two hundred yards and squeezed the trigger. At the shot the buck put on a burst of speed like I have never seen in an animal, telling me that I probably missed. Then, he was suddenly tumbling in the brush. As day turned to night, we found the buck in the sage. It was the first time that I had seen an antelope up close and I admired the features and markings on the speedster.

This bonus speedster was taken before the author's hunt was even scheduled to begin.

The next day, actually the first real day of my hunt, we hunted the main ranch. We saw several bucks, but nothing very big. Les thought he saw a good buck, but it turned out to be a massive shed antler positioned in a perfect manner to entice an embarrassing stalk. In one spot, we were sitting on some high ground, glassing the surrounding area when we noticed some movement down the ridgeline. The movement soon became a cow and calf elk, and following them was a very nice 6x6 elk. They passed within about fifty yards as I busily snapped pictures. Les remarked that for the few elk hunters they'd have on the ranch that year, that particular bull would not have been a shooter. I shook my head in disbelief, as we continued down the ridge. The rest of the day was very enjoyable, but no big bucks made an appearance.... for me anyway.

When we got back to camp we found that a group of new hunters had come in to camp, and while they were waiting for their luggage to arrive, one of them set up a spotting scope and started glassing the surrounding area. He spotted a massive buck about a half mile away, and when his gun arrived, he and his guide headed for the buck. After a good stalk, he put the buck down. He was huge, with several trash points and approaching two hundred inches.

The next day we jumped into the truck and headed for a different ranch. Very much like the previous day, we started working from knoll to knoll, glassing as we went. We were above a heavily timbered area when antlers flashed in the sun. A good buck was making his way through the trees. As much as I tried, I couldn't get a good look at him. Later in the day I spotted a good buck breaking over a knoll and raced up the side to see if I could get a shot at him. I reached the top with Les right behind and got into a sitting position. That's about the time I found out there were cactus in Wyoming. The buck disappeared into the wood line before I could get on him. The rest of the afternoon passed uneventfully until we were driving out. I spotted a group of does and a very good buck on the skyline. Les and I bailed out of the truck and raced down into a valley and up to the other side of the hill to try and get a shot, but they were gone by the time we got there.

The third day was clear and brisk with a steady wind blowing from the northwest. We went right back to the same ranch. We worked the ridges and valleys, slipping along into the wind using every opportunity to glass. We saw several does and small bucks, but no shooters. As we were headed back to the truck there was one small drainage that we had not worked. Even though it looked like the brush was short and we should be able to see anything in the area, Les decided we should try it.

As we eased slowly along the slope all of a sudden a buck and a few does boiled out of their beds right under Les's feet like a covey of quail. A quick glance was all he needed. He dove to the side yelling, "Shoot! Shoot!" The buck ran down the drainage flat out and I struggled to catch up to him in the scope. Just before he went around the bend I got everything aligned and dropped the hammer. The buck disappeared and I thought I had missed. I turned to Les who said, "What a shot." Slightly confused, I asked him what he meant, and he said, "You got him." I couldn't believe it. We walked down into the gully and down to the bluff and there he was, a beautiful 4x4.

The author and guide Les Snodgrass busted this buck out of cover that would barely hide a rabbit.

I spent the next few days wandering around the ranch taking pictures and gathering shed antlers. It was a great hunt and to this day the smell of sage takes me right back to Wyoming.

Chapter 17
Way Out There
1978–2001

"How far?" I asked settling in behind the bipod. "Five hundred," my guide replied. I quickly figured the twenty-six inches of drop, brought the crosshairs over the buck's back and squeezed the trigger. I was in the mountains of Idaho, a long way from the heavy brush of central New York, and a long time from humble beginnings.

My first gun to be used for deer hunting was a pump twelve gauge JC Higgins that my grandfather had. It had a smooth bore full choke and a bead the size of a marble on the end of the barrel. It was the same gun my father used when he began deer hunting. It also explains why he never came back with anything. Not knowing any better I think my sighting in consisted of a paper plate at some indeterminate distance, probably close enough to throw a cow pie. Once the plate was hit, and the Kentucky windage computed, it was time to go hunting. This really wasn't as bad as it sounds, since most of our shooting would be well under fifty yards. Okay, yes, it was as bad as it sounds, but we didn't know any better.

The biggest issue that was impressed on me even before I started deer hunting was that when you were shooting those one ounce hunks of lead, they were very slow and had a serious rainbow trajectory. It became so engrained in my mind that I could almost see them barely making it out of the barrel. They were obviously going so slow that they would be skipping across the ground within a few short yards. Armed with this knowledge wedged firmly in what ever passes for a brain in a teenager I hit the woods for my first deer hunt.

The first few days passed without any opportunity for a shot. Although our little group almost never did any driving, nothing was moving so on the third day we decided to make a small push. I was placed on a hedgerow next to a field of perhaps ten acres. I had just gotten set up when a doe burst out of the thick stuff right in front of me, and stopped facing me head on. With the rainbow trajectory fully programmed in my head, I aimed over her head and squeezed the trigger figuring that the slug would drop into her neck. I watched in disbelief as she just stood there. I racked in another shell and sent another mortar over her head. She got the picture with this one and kicked into overdrive. In retrospect, she probably wasn't much over twenty or thirty yards.

Then something much, much worse happened. The most precious critter in New York popped out of the hedgerow, an actual real live buck. Fortunately for him, he came out further away than the doe, requiring me to aim even further toward the heavens. I managed to lob a half dozen slugs over his back as he ran across the field. I was shaking like a leaf and couldn't believe that I hadn't connected. That was the beginning of my hate/hate relationship with slug guns.

I talked about my first deer and first buck previously. Both of those deer were actually taken with the same weapon. However, before that season, I actually spent some time shooting the gun at known ranges and found out exactly where it would shoot. It still was about as accurate as a full choke pump shotgun, but at least I had a better idea of what I was doing.

That Remington 1100 that I bought with my earnings from the vineyard work was the next step up in slug guns, and I figured for sure that it would be a more accurate weapon. It was, but I think that was only because it had a modified choke and a smaller bead than the Higgins. I did manage to take a good buck with it though. I was set up in my trusty Baker climbing tree stand in a narrow stretch of woods that acted like a funnel for the deer. Gun season in central New York means there are a lot of hunters in the woods and the pressure is on. This funnel served as a perfect escape path, and I used it frequently. This particular morning was dreary and cool with a slight drizzle. It was mid morning and I had only seen a few does tiptoe by. Then I heard a branch crack up in the woods that put me on full alert. A few seconds later I could hear something crashing towards me at a fast pace. A huge buck (any buck that was more than six points was huge back then) burst out of the cover at a fast trot and quickly closed the distance to thirty yards in a heartbeat. Out of instinct more than real aiming I swung the barrel on him like a grouse and pulled the trigger. He collapsed, skidded five yards and laid there without moving.

I set a record for Baker stand dismounts, leaving nothing but a skid mark on the tree, and hurried over to the buck. He was the best buck I had seen with a gun in my hands and I couldn't wait to get my father and uncle.

Shortly after that, in search of better accuracy, I bought a slug barrel for the 1100 figuring that it would increase my accuracy ten fold. Well, with a slug barrel slid into place it certainly did better than the JC Higgins or the modified barrel. An actual sight was a welcome change from the bead, but it still was realistically only a fifty yard gun, shooting groups the size of a pie plate at that distance.

I figured what I really needed was a scope. Dad heard about a mounting system that was available for the 1100. So I bought a scope, and a mounting system that attached to the side of the gun, using the pins that hold the action in place. The flaw in the system was that if you over tightened the bolts, the action would freeze up and you were left with a single shot shotgun. For what ever reason, I never had a lot of luck with this system. It seemed like I'd get it zeroed on one day and the next it would be off. Or I'd get it shooting well, make a bad hit on a deer and find out that it was shooting eight inches to the left.

From there, I got a Remington 870, with a slug barrel and a pistol scope mounted right on the barrel. I had similar problems with this gun. It seemed like I could shoot a three inch group at fifty yards and then spray one almost off the paper with a good trigger pull. To this day, I don't know what the story was with me and slug guns, but it always seemed like something would always go wrong. I had been hunting with slug guns for several years when the following incident occurred. I was hunting a permanent tree stand that I had built. It was one of those perfect fall days that we all live for. It was sunny but cool, there was a steady but light breeze from the west and the leaves were crispy and dry. I had been sitting there for several hours with nothing moving when I heard steps in the leaves. A nice eight point cautiously made his way down a trail that would pass within thirty yards of me. I slowly got my gun into position, and waited for the perfect moment to squeeze the trigger. At thirty yards, I centered the crosshairs on his chest and squeezed the trigger. It was a slam dunk shot.

I waited for twenty minutes and went down to track the buck. Normally it helps to have blood to track a buck. There was none. How about some hair to indicate the location of the hit? Nope, not a thing. I even followed the running buck's tracks in the leaves for a while to see if I could find blood. Then I walked some half circles further out, to see if I could find some blood. Finally I climbed back up into the stand to see if I could see anything from there.

What I saw was a chunk taken out of the side of a tree. This particular tree was not even close to the buck when I shot. My gun was shooting a full eighteen inches off at that range. It had not been dropped, in fact it had been treated like fine china since I had verified its zero a few days previously. Everything was still tight as well. That episode ended my slug gun hunting, I had had enough of those types of experiences so I just called it quits. From then on, when I was in the southern tier, it was either a muzzle loader or a pistol.

Somewhere in the early eighties the deer population in upstate New York, and specifically around my house started to become noticeable. I decided that a real rifle was in order. I went to a gun shop looking mainly for something cheap. I certainly got it. There was a sporterized military .303 British sitting there with a very low tag on it. Not having a clue what I was doing, I asked about the cartridge and was assured that it would work fine on deer. Soon I was walking out of the shop with the rifle in hand. It probably shot a six inch group at a hundred yards and had a trigger that you had to sneak up on to make it go bang. But, again, not knowing any better I thought I had a tremendous step up from my experiences with the slug guns. I never did shoot a deer with that gun, but did wander through the woods with it a time or two.

Then we get to the point where my views on shooting changed drastically. I had just gotten out of college and actually had a steady paycheck coming in. My priorities were in order, and I had not given myself a graduation present, so my first real purchase was going to be a 30-06 rifle. I had done some research and decided that if I could only get one rifle, this caliber would give me the most versatility. Money of course was an issue, but with my experience with the .303 British, I wanted a name brand. I ended up with a Remington 700 ADL, put a cheap scope on it, adjusted the trigger to an unknown but light amount and headed for the range (actually my parent's back yard).

Right away I knew I was dealing with something entirely different. I didn't know about the differences in ammunition back then so I was using the cheap stuff. Even so, the accuracy I was getting was very impressive. An inch and a half group at a hundred yards seemed like a laser compared to what I was used to. I had always read about guys making three and four hundred yard shots, and based on my experiences I just found that hard to believe. This gun would change my mind in a big way.

Several months after that, I was wandering through a gun shop the way teenage girls wander through the mall, and saw a used Thompson Contender pistol in .35 Remington sitting there. It looked lonely, so I decided to give it a good home. Whoever owned it before me had set it up with a light trigger, and a two and a half power scope. The first time I shot it was quite a shock to my hands, and I wasn't expecting the huge ball of fire that erupted from the barrel, but I quickly got the hang of it. Again, even using cheap ammunition, the accuracy was astounding. It was not unusual for me to print one inch groups at a hundred yards with that pistol.

Over a short time I found that the Thompson Contender was still lonely, so I also bought a Browning lever action in .243. My next big step in the right direction was when I took that rifle with two others, and several different brands of ammunition out and ran some comparisons. I did my test shooting at two hundred yards since that's where I was zeroing the rifles at that time. The results were staggering, and consistent. One particular brand (whom will remain nameless) consistently produced groups that were as much as double the other brands. Federal Premium came out on top for each rifle, and I gave the other brands away.

It was also about this time that I realized the difference in shooting light crisp triggers and a factory set trigger like the Browning still possessed. It was obvious to me right off the bat that accurate shooting demanded a light trigger, period. The Browning made a quick trip to the gunsmith to rectify that situation. A few years back I had a friend up at the range, sighting in a new rifle and he was having some trouble. I asked if I could give it a try. I guess it's a result of lawsuits, but that trigger was set so high I practically needed to brace my feet against the edge of the deck and pull with both hands. It was like trying to perform neurosurgery wearing boxing gloves. I told him that he needed to get to gunsmith before he sprained his trigger finger.

I started shooting at longer ranges. Through trial and error I worked on what to do and what not to do when shooting to produce consistently good groups. I found during these sessions that the Remington shot about nine inches low at three hundred yards, and still shot good groups. At four hundred yards it was dropping like a rock, but still shooting decent groups. With Federal Premium ammunition, that gun would shoot inside minute of angle, every single time. I hunted with that gun successfully for several years and still take it out with me when long range shots will not be presented. To this day, that cheap Remington is my most accurate rifle. On one trip with that rifle, we were at the range making sure the scopes were still on before starting a hunt on the following day. I placed a group on paper at a hundred yards in a perfect cloverleaf. It was a group of perhaps three eighths of an inch. The outfitter asked me how much I wanted for the gun. I told him with a grin that it wasn't for sale. It would have been interesting to see how high he was willing to go.

My next step up in long range shooting was when I was preparing for my first trip to Alaska for caribou. The Browning A-Bolts with the BOSS (Ballistic Optimizing Shooting System) were relatively new and were getting good reviews so I decided on that weapon. As for a caliber, I wanted something that was accurate, that I could use for bigger game and something that would reach out and touch something. After some research, I settled on the .300 Win Mag.

I also decided that since I'd be hunting in some extreme conditions, it needed to be stainless as well. Since this gun was going to be my primary long range weapon, I topped it with a 4-12 Leupold scope.

Once I got the gun home, I did some experimentation with the BOSS and got it dialed in to produce minute of angle or better groups. The BOSS also incorporated a recoil reducer. Even with earplugs it sounded very loud, so I normally wore foam ear plugs in my ears and a set of muffs when shooting. On that Alaskan caribou hunt described earlier I had managed to lose an earplug and ended up shooting with a plug in only my left ear. At the shot, I honestly thought I had seriously damaged my right eardrum. It was an experience I decided never to repeat. I ended up ordering a solid BOSS. Once I had that in place, life got much better with that gun. The recoil isn't that bad, and the noise is greatly reduced.

For the actual zeroing of the gun, I first zeroed it at two hundred and fifty yards, but with some experimentation settled on a zero of three hundred yards. I was never a person that would sight in two inches high at a hundred yards and go hunting. I always zero the gun at the actual zero yardage, then shoot further and shorter to establish the real trajectory of the bullet/gun combination. In the case of the .300 Win Mag, shooting a hundred and eighty grain Nosler partitions, a three hundred yard zero resulted in being about four inches high at one hundred and two hundred fifty yards, and six inches high at a hundred fifty, and two hundred yards. The gun would shoot a foot low at four hundred yards and about twenty-six inches low at five hundred yards. Those trajectories were ingrained in my head, and at known ranges and a good rest I felt like I could take anything inside of five hundred yards.

In my preparation for the Alaskan hunt, I also did some shooting duplicating field conditions. The first thing that became apparent was that a very solid steady rest was required, even from the more steady positions. I bought a Harris bipod, and it's the best purchase I've made for field condition shooting. I've heard people say that they don't like them because they add weight to the rifle, but in my mind they're cheap, light insurance of a good rest. I also found that realistically, I was not a very good off hand shot and anything much over a hundred yards was probably safe. All the more reason to ensure a good rest was present.

A few years ago, Leupold came out with the B&C reticle that has multiple crosshairs and ten mile an hour windage indicators. It's a great concept, so I purchased a 4.5-14 power scope with that feature. I'm sure they recommended something different in the directions, but a real man doesn't need directions so I headed for the range for some experimentation. I found that with the second reticle sighted dead on at three hundred yards, the top reticle is about dead on at a hundred fifty yards. In essence the top reticle is dead on out to two hundred yards for deer sized game. The four hundred through five hundred yard reticles are about dead on as well with my rifle. This completely eliminates guess work on hold over at known ranges. I have since taken that rifle to the far corners of the world, I've had it out in sweltering heat and sub zero cold. I've abused it mercilessly and it has the scars to prove it. It's seen more rain, sleet and snow than my mailman and yet at the moment of truth, it always comes through for me. What a difference from those old slug guns I started with.

All of this led me to a mountain in northern Idaho described earlier, faced with what we later determined to be just under a five hundred yard shot. As I squeezed the trigger, I lost sight of the buck with the recoil, but the shot felt solid. This was confirmed when my guide exclaimed, "What a shot!" as the nice 5x5 buck tumbled down the side of the mountain. Was it luck? Maybe a little, but I like to think that it was the culmination of years of trial and error, along with a healthy dose of preparation.

This nice Idaho 5x5 was taken at long range with a flat shooting accurate rifle and a solid rest.

During my South African trip we were riding around looking for a steinbuck one evening. It was warm and clear and we were in fairly open terrain. After about an hour we spotted a small herd of fallow deer out in the open. The deer generally stayed on another piece of property where they had been released several years earlier. Nasie, whose property we were hunting and the other landowner had an agreement that if they wandered on to Nasie's property, he could go ahead and take one if he wanted. The problem was that they were way out there and Nasie didn't think he could make the shot. My Professional Hunter Ian told Nasie that I could make the shot, but it would ruin the steinbuck hunt. I agreed to forego the steinbuck hunt and settled into a prone position. Our range finders weren't reading all the way to the buck, so the best we could figure, he was just under four hundred yards. I squeezed the trigger and the sound of a hit reverberated back to us. I must admit to a few follow up shots, but my first shot had caught the back of the lungs and he was done. Quite a difference from lobbing slugs over a doe's head at thirty yards just a few short years before.

Author with a fallow deer taken in South Africa "way out there".

Chapter 18

Flatland Elk, Believe It Or Not

2000

I met outfitter Randy Christensen, guide Art Warren and his brother Bob just outside Golden, Colorado. A few last minute supplies were picked up and we were off for southern Colorado. We drove south for several hours along the edge of the Rocky Mountains, which I enjoy so much. The difference for this trip however is that as we approached our hunting area we turned east instead of west. Randy had explained that through the years, the elk population in the plains east of the mountains had been expanding, and was now very huntable. I looked around and saw the sweetest sight I've seen when hunting. Flat. Nothing but flat ground as far as the eye could see. We pulled into Randy's parents place, introductions were made and we got settled in. We would be hunting a few of the local ranches that Randy had access to, and I was looking forward to the lack of elevation and shear cliffs.

The first morning out we were driving across a field toward our intended hunting area when suddenly there were elk in front of us. It was still early as I bailed out of the truck, pulled out my bipod and got into a sitting position. Randy quickly glassed the elk and pronounced the bull running to our right to be a shooter. I clicked off the safety and followed the animal till he stopped. In the low light, I couldn't tell if there was another elk directly behind him, so I held off on the shot. The bull soon got tired of our foolishness and disappeared into the woods.

We glassed a few areas with no luck, and were on our way back to the truck when a cow call filtered through the morning air. Then a shrill bugle echoed out from the forest. We were on the edge of a field and it appeared that a herd was working its way toward us. I laid on my belly on the frozen ground and searched the woods for movement across three hundred yards of field. As we waited, Art asked if I wanted to get closer. I was prone with a bipod, so I told him I was okay. Besides, I think I was frozen to the ground, at least the whole front of my body was frozen. We waited for what seemed like hours and finally caught movement in the trees. Some cows drifted through, and we waited for the bull. He never showed, apparently having plans elsewhere.

That evening a group of us was walking toward a large field, when the sounds of elk reached our ears. Soon we came to a spot where we could see some through a small opening. I handed my rangefinder to Marty as we crept forward. The elk must have seen us, because we were busted as we came around the corner. I immediately dropped into a prone position and Randy glassed the herd as they broke into the open. Suddenly a massive body flashed into the open attached to a nice rack. Randy told me to take him, and I asked Marty for the range. He replied that it was three hundred, even though he later told me it was only two ninety-five. It's hard to get good help these days.

I watched a cow clear as she ran away out of the edge of the scope, centered the crosshairs and squeezed the trigger. The bull whirled and ran for the trees along a river bottom before I could get another shot off. Randy asked if I hit him, and I told him that the hold felt good. We went over and started looking for blood. Not a drop was found. We circled that area until it simply got too dark to see, and decided to come back in the morning.

That was a long night, as I kept repeating the shot in my head. It always came out the same way, it felt like I had done everything right. The next morning we started looking in the field and then progressed into he woods. I could tell that the guys were starting to doubt a hit. I was walking along some brush, when Randy called me over. He told me that he had found the bull, and he was still alive. He was also on another person's property. He went back to the truck to phone the landowner, and then signaled that it was okay to finish him off. The bull was bedded in the riverbed with his head up, but obviously not going anywhere. Unbelievably, Art and I could clearly see that he was shot exactly through the center of both lungs. After Randy signaled, I placed the crosshairs behind his shoulder and squeezed the trigger. At the shot, the bull leapt to his feet and headed across the river. I quickly shot again and he came to a halt in the center of the river. Another shot and he finally fell.

The top picture shows the author wading out into the river to retrieve the bull, ignoring the laughter on the shoreline. The bottom picture shows the bull with from left to right, the author, Randy Christensen, and Art Warren.

Randy was back at the truck wondering what the heck was going on, and started back to see what the firefight was all about. We related the story, and then started to talk about how we were going to get him out of there. Either I volunteered or was volunteered to wade out into the river with a rope to tie to the bull's antlers so we could haul him to shore. As the water topped my boots, and the ice cold water poured in I held my breath until the pain started to fade and continued to wade towards the bull. I tied the rope around the bull's antlers ignoring the laughter from shore. Someone must have told a joke or something ...

I got back to shore and we all grabbed the rope and pulled. I was amazed at how much the bull weighed, and the amount of effort required getting the partially buoyant beast to shore. We finally got him on dry ground, and started to look him over. My original shot had been text book. What was not, was the bullet's performance. I had found a name brand ammunition specifically made for elk sized animals and was using it for the first time. The bullet had punched through without expanding, and the damage was minimal. The bull had also not left a drop of blood, except for a small amount right in his bed. The bull had wire wrapped around the base of his antlers so tightly that it had cut off the blood supply and the antlers had not developed fully, with the top still being in dry hard velvet.

We got the bull gutted, loaded him up on a four wheeler (don't ask how), put a person on the back of the four wheeler to keep the back wheels on the ground, and Marty headed back with slightly over the recommended weight limit. We got back to Randy's parents place and pulled the bull up with a front end loader to begin skinning operations. I could not believe the size of the bull's body as the loader pulled him higher and higher.

We got the bull to the local butcher, and I stayed around a few days to help the guys fill their tags. Then, I completely loaded up the back of my truck with coolers, meat and dry ice and headed for home, another adventure safe and snug in my memory.

Chapter 19
South Africa Adventure
2001

I heard some noise, perhaps the clattering of rocks several hundred yards away through the impenetrable mass of thorn laden brush and cactus. After a lifetime of shooting, my Professional Hunter Ian Hendry couldn't quite make it out. A few minutes passed and I thought maybe I was mistaken, when I heard some more noise. Something was definitely making its way towards us. A few moments later I caught movement on the hillside, perhaps three hundred yards in front of us. Two Kudu bulls were busting their way towards us at a trot.

I was on a hunt of a lifetime. My first trip to Africa, and I was about to encounter one of the coolest creatures to roam the earth. I grew up reading magazines like Outdoor Life, Sports Afield and Field and Stream. I was always fascinated with articles about animals that I simply could not even dream about hunting. Sheep, elk, African animals and other exotics filled my imagination with hunts in far off lands. I remember reading an excerpt from Peter Hathaway Capstick's <u>Death in the Long Grass</u> when I was a kid and being fascinated by the prose. Several years later, when I had settled into my first job, I happened to run across the book for sale and immediately ordered a copy. I devoured the book, reading for hours straight. I followed that up by ordering everything I could get my hands on by Peter. Then, I anxiously awaited each additional book that he produced.

More than anything else, Peter's writing instilled a burning desire to experience Africa and has had a sever impact on my bank account ever since. I always wanted to meet him so I could impart the blame appropriately. I was greatly saddened by his passing. Over the years, I've read works by other authors of course, but nothing compared to that initial jolt of Peter's work.

I had already broken the ice with other outfitted hunts, and was researching various African hunts when I stumbled across an off season plains game safari to South Africa. Now, "off season" to me meant "cheaper". I was told that it also meant "hotter", but I figured I could stand about anything to be able to experience a trip to Africa. I booked the hunt about a year ahead of time, which gave me plenty of time to figure out what I was getting myself into, and study things like which snakes could kill me and how fast I would die. Before I left on the trip, a friend asked if I was taking snake boots. I told him that it wouldn't do much good since there were snakes over there that could look you in the eye, and all snake boots would do is slow me down.

In practically no time it was March of 2001 and I found myself on a plane from Syracuse, NY to New York, NY and then from there, a fourteen and a half hour trip to Johannesburg (seventeen and a half hours on the way back). Then from Johannesburg I took a flight to Port Elizabeth, barely making the connection after completing the necessary paperwork for my rifles. I was picked up in Port Elizabeth along with several other hunters and driven to the base camp of John X Safaris. From my doorstep, to my well outfitted hut ended up being about forty two hours of travel.

I was introduced to my Professional Hunter, Ian Hendry, a resident of South Africa. Ian is an easy going person, with a wealth of knowledge about the flora and fauna of Africa. He was born and raised in Kenya and moved to South Africa in 1963. We hit it off immediately, and sat down at the bar to discuss my hunt. Of course March in upstate New York is somewhat cooler than South Africa in March, so I mostly sat at the bar and sweated in the hot humid night air. Ian asked me what my priorities were for the hunt. I told him that more than anything, I wanted to take a kudu. Everything else was secondary, though I think I put the gemsbok second. Ian set about making arrangements to head for other camps, and said we'd spend the first day hunting mountain reedbuck on John X's property. Other than looking up what a mountain reedbuck was in my National Audubon Society Field Guide to African Wildlife, I really had no idea what kind of an animal it was, and to be honest didn't really care if I got one or not. It didn't matter to me though, I was finally going to be able to hunt in Africa. I went back to my hut and got settled in for the night, trying to ignore the salad plate sized spiders on the walls.

First thing in the morning, I was introduced to tracker and skinner Pearce, and we headed out to make sure my Browning Stainless Stalker was still on. I was once again shooting my .300 Winchester Magnum with a four to twelve Leupold scope that I had zeroed at three hundred yards. I had a Harris bipod and as I've said previously, I had shot the gun so much that I knew the bullet trajectories out to five hundred yards by heart and could instantly adjust the crosshairs for any range. With a Bushnell rangefinder on my belt, I was ready to go hunt mountain reedbuck, what ever they were.

We started down a trail, found a good vantage point and glassed the surrounding brushy hills. It was pretty much standard mule deer procedure. I love spot and stalk hunting, so this was right up my alley. The difference was that I've never seen a baboon or a zebra while mule deer hunting. We saw a good amount of game including some mountain reedbucks. They're small animals, probably sixty to eighty pounds live weight with a brownish rust color coat and small forward curving horns. I found their behavior to be very much like whitetails, being shy animals and liking heavy cover. Some of the females and small rams (bucks?, bulls?) would let you get a good look at them, but any of the mature males were gone in a flash. One interesting experience we had involved a female mountain reedbuck. We were driving around the corner of a hill and she was bedded in the grass just above the trail. As soon as she saw us, she flattened her head to the ground and disappeared. She let us get close enough for a nice close up picture before she bolted for cover.

I started the day not caring much about shooting a mountain reedbuck, and ended it without a mountain reedbuck and wanting very much to shoot one. Even though we didn't get anything, I felt that the first day was an incredible success. We saw plenty of animals and experienced a great day of viewing wildlife. It did heat up pretty good during the middle of the day, but we simply headed back to camp and waited a few hours for the sun to start its downward path, and journeyed back out again. This is pretty much the standard pattern for hunting Africa when the heat is turned up.

Ian decided to cover a different area for the second day, and right off the bat we walked into a herd of blesbok. Now I knew what a blesbok was. They're about the size of a young midwestern whitetail. They're a dark brown color with a white blaze running down the length of their nose. They've got curved horns generally ranging right around thirteen to sixteen inches. What I didn't know about blesbok was what a good one looked like on the hoof.

We were quietly sneaking along a brushy hillside when Ian suddenly froze. We had walked right up to the unsuspecting herd only fifty yards or so directly in front of us. As Ian began to glass the herd, one of the females decided something was amiss and took the rest of the herd with her. Ian knew the country and we made a half circle of about a quarter mile, ending up on a hillside overlooking a large open field. We spotted a group, but they were too far away for a shot. Ian however confirmed that there were a few good males in the group, and explained that I should first look for the white fronts on the horns as an indication of age. After waiting a while, a good ram worked his way into range. Ian asked if I could take him, and I confirmed that at two hundred and sixty five yards and a good rest, it shouldn't be a problem. Having been a professional hunter for many years, Ian always had a back up gun on hand, for clients who might be a little too excited and make a bad hit. I noticed him getting ready for this possibility, as I settled in behind the scope.

I steadied the crosshairs just a little low and squeezed the pound and a half trigger. The gun jumped in my hands, and the resounding thump of a hit echoed back across the hillside. The ram ran twenty yards and stopped. "Hit him again," Ian whispered anxiously. I was just about to do so, when he spun around and fell to the ground. My first African animal had just been taken, and I was on cloud nine. We walked down to the ram, and I marveled at the coloration and the thick horns. After congratulations, pictures were taken, and we let Pearce get to work skinning the animal. We then returned to the base camp.

The Author and PH Ian Hendry with a nice bull blesbok, the author's first African animal.

The afternoon was spent pursuing those little mountain reedbuck sons of.... uh, guns. But again, they eluded us, though we got to look over some new territory and see some more game. We were severely scolded by some baboons and

I got to hear the call of the Honey Guide Bird, and successfully resisted the urge to follow him to the hive.

Ian had me get packed up, and early the third morning in the predawn darkness we were on the road to the Great Karoo in the Cape Province. Along the way we passed through the Addo Elephant National Park. We hit one section of road just in time to have a white rhino bull step out in front of us. Then a cow and calf made an appearance. It's hard to believe just how big they are until you're face to face with one at about twenty yards. The bull literally took up the entire roadway. Following that bit of excitement, we traveled for several hours taking us from the relatively green coastal area to a hotter more arid region of South Africa.

This is a big bull white rhino stepping out into the road. He had the right of way.

We arrived at a lodge owned by Noel and Jan Ross, got settled in and headed for the hills to hunt for kudu and reedbuck. Shortly after heading into the bush, we stopped and began glassing a hillside. Ian explained that in this region where the cover alternates between being relatively open, to dense thickets, it's generally a good bet that the kudu would be found in the thick stuff. All of a sudden two kudu bulls burst from the cover. Ian gave them a quick glance and told me not to shoot, they were too young. I really didn't care, I had finally seen a kudu in the wild, what could be better than that? We saw a few more kudu during the rest of the afternoon, along with some of the elusive mountain reedbucks, but nothing big enough or stationary enough to shoot.

Late in the afternoon, we heard from Noel that he had spotted a group of bachelor bulls on a hillside and there were a few shooters in the group. As we headed towards that location we came upon a large group of impala and made a quick stalk to see if there were any big males in the group. We ended up spooking them before we could see all of them but from what we could see it was a group of females and young. Ian said that there was probably a big male in the group but he'd rather not shoot it since it had been shown to affect the breeding capability within the herd. We made it to the bottom of the hill where Noel was and headed up the slope as the light quickly faded. We made it up the hill and could see the bulls feeding through the brush about a hundred and fifty yards out. As Ian and Noel tried to determine which bull was the best, the light continued to drop, and after a while it was simply too dark to make a shot. We headed back down the hill to the lodge, and some wildebeest steaks awaiting us.

On the fourth day we continued to hunt kudu and those mysterious mountain reedbucks. We saw a few cow kudu and some more mountain reedbucks, but it was more of the same. Each time we saw a decent male, he'd be running the other way in a heart beat and disappear into the brush. Then, one waited just a bit too long. We were working our way around a large gently sloping hill and spotted a few of them up near the top. Ian pronounced the male a good one, but he was headed away, a familiar sight. I slapped down the bipod, quickly ranged him at three hundred and thirty five yards and settled in behind the scope. By the time I got on him he was quartering away and had slowed to a walk. I placed the crosshairs a little high and squeezed the trigger.

At the shot I lost the sight picture and turned to Ian, and said, "Miss?" He turned to me with a grin and said, "I think you got him, he disappeared at the shot." Pearce headed up the hill and pretty soon we were looking at what for me was the most elusive creature in Africa. I'm forever grateful to Ian for having me hunt those hillside Houdini's.

Once we took care of the reedbuck, Ian got word that Noel had spotted a good kudu on a hillside. We got to where he was, sitting behind a spotting scope. He was staring up an especially arid looking hill about a half mile away and said that there was a good bull in the scant cover. We discussed the wind and the terrain and decided that we had to approach from above. We drove a long way around the hill and got as close as we could by Land cruiser. Then we walked up the backside of the hill, just over the top to a rocky outcropping, overlooking the area where the bull was. The rocks had been baking in the sun all day and were about the temperature of lava, but we got settled in and began to glass. After an hour, we had picked apart every thorn laden bush in the area and could not locate the bull. We decided to ease down the hill and see if we could kick him out. Over the next half hour we tiptoed down the hill to no avail, he had simply disappeared. I guess that's why they're called the gray ghost.

The author may not have known what a mountain reedbuck was when he arrived in South Africa, but he got an education quickly.

We spent the morning of the fifth day chasing kudu around some more, but they were on to us and we didn't see a single bull. We made our way to Nasie and Renel Vermaak's place, got settled in and headed out to try something different. That "something different" was gemsbok and springbok and any of the smaller antelope we happened to see. We headed out into a fairly flat area at the base of a huge ridgeline that ran as far as you could see. Much of the area was open grassland interspersed with brush and trees. Ian explained that the springbok males will claim a chunk of ground and defend it against all rivals. The females weren't necessarily tied to a male and could actually wander from one territory to another.

Nasie knew the property, and accompanied us on the hunt. There were springbok everywhere. They're a beautiful little antelope, with a tan coat with white and dark patches. We alternately drove and glassed, looking for a good ram. We parked in one spot and walked up on top of a hill. The wind was kicking up and the sun was fading fast as we approached the summit.

Before I even got settled in, Ian said, "Can you hit that one right in front of us?" I looked down the hill and saw a springbok standing head on looking at us. I ranged him quickly at just under two hundred yards and got into a prone position. The wind was blowing very hard right up the hill but I felt steady enough to make the shot. The ram collapsed at the squeeze of the trigger. As we walked down to the ram Nasie said that he was neck shot, which I couldn't imagine. We headed down to the ram, and sure enough, I had caught him low in the neck. I immediately realized that I was visualizing a whitetail as I positioned the crosshairs, not an animal less than half that size. That mature springbok might have weighed eighty pounds soaking wet. The six inches low that I thought I was aiming wasn't even close on the tiny antelope. I actually should have held the crosshairs just under the hair line to allow the bullet to pass through the vitals. It was a lesson learned that I applied in the days to follow.

The next day dawned especially steamy and we headed out to see about getting a shot at a gemsbok. Nasie also said that with the neck shot on the previous day's springbok, I should make a rug out of that one, and take another for a shoulder mount should the opportunity arise. That sounded like a good plan to me, so off we went. Somewhere around this part of the journey, we saw the snake. That was a bad thing since I had almost forgotten about all the reptiles inhabiting that part of the world. The worse thing was the size of the bloody thing. We saw a puff adder lying beside a trail minding his own business. As we walked up to it, I was shocked at how big it was. It was probably just under three feet in length, but as big around as my arm. The head was massive and you could easily make out the telltale venom sacks on either side of its head. When I lifted him up, he felt like he weighed at least five pounds. Just kidding, no way I was touching that beast. He probably would have wrestled me to the ground and beaten me. I couldn't imagine what kind of a punch it would be to get hit by something like that. Oh yeah, and then there's that "venom" thing too.

So off we went, with me thinking about snakes and scorpions and millipedes.... We hadn't gone far when Ian spotted a mature springbok with fairly narrow horns, a perfect candidate. I ranged him at two hundred and eighty five yards, settled in and squeezed the trigger. The ram collapsed at the shot. After the congratulations and pictures, we loaded him up and headed back to the lodge to get him skinned out. Then we rode back out to see about getting a gemsbok. I've heard references to the "clown face" of the gemsbok, but to me they're a very handsome looking antelope, with very striking black and white blaze marks on their faces and a nice light brown coat. They tend to live in open country, and as such we spotted a herd fairly quickly. We circled with the wind and quickly got into position for a shot a few hundred yards away. Nasie and Ian found a big bull in the herd and pointed it out to me. Just as I was about to shoot the herd spooked, and we were left looking at a cloud of dust. After a while, they settled down and we circled around ahead of them. We called it perfectly and they walked right past us at a hundred and thirty five yards. I placed the crosshairs behind the shoulder of the big bull and squeezed the trigger. Soon he was down and we walked up to the beautiful animal. We took some pictures and loaded him into the truck for the trip back to camp.

One of Africa's finest looking animals, a nice bull gemsbok.

The next day we went to a different area to try our hands at kudu again. It was going to be a different sort of hunt with several people driving around to the back side of a mountain, and trying to drive the kudu down the center of the drainage we were overlooking. It sounded like an interesting plan, and in no time we were set up on the hillside waiting for the action to start.

After about forty minutes of sitting, the sounds of hooves and clattering rocks echoed through the valley. As I readied myself for the dozens of kudu that were making their way toward me, I could see movement in the brush. A lone zebra trotted out of the bush and right towards us. As he got closer, Ian identified it as a mountain zebra, which were quite rare in the area. We got a good look, since he came within about ten yards of us. That was the only animal we saw, the kudu evidently had plans elsewhere.

It was around this point that I realized Ian wasn't carrying a backup rifle anymore. I took it as a compliment as we headed back to Noel's place to try for Kudu some more. We were driving on the side of a long hill, looking at the valley down below. After some glassing, we saw a herd of impala rams filtering through the cover several hundred yards below. We walked down the road and then entered the bush in the last direction we saw them. The ground was very dry and the leaves sounded like we were walking on potato chips. We walked very slowly and hoped that the rams would think that we were just tall impala. After twenty minutes or so, we saw movement thirty yards out through the impenetrable thorns. We continued forward, glassing as we went, trying to determine if there was a shooter in there anywhere. Ultimately, the cover was too thick, it was too dry and we had to get too close to the rams to see them. We ended up spooking them and they ran down the hill.

We walked back to the truck, made a huge circle around the hill and came in a half mile below the spot we spooked the rams. The hillside wasn't quite as dense as it was further up and Ian felt sure that they'd continue down the hill. We waited for fifteen minutes and it was beginning to look like they had gone elsewhere, when we spotted movement up the slope. They had settled down, and were actually feeding again, slowly moving down the hill. Finally a good ram stepped into a clearing just over two hundred yards away. I was already on the bipod, when Ian asked me if I could take him.

With my experience overshooting the bushbuck fresh in my mind, I settled the crosshairs right on the hairline at the bottom of his chest to allow for shooting six inches high at that range. I squeezed the trigger and thought I heard the thump of the bullet striking true. We walked to the clearing, and shortly found a blood trail. Ian and Pearce started on the trail and we had only gone a short distance when Ian said something to Pearce. I found ourselves leaving the blood trail and asked what was going on. I was told that this is the way we track in Africa. I took one look over to the blood trail, and said, "Okay, when in Rome …" That one glance showed me the impala that was laying a few yards away in the brush, and Ian chuckling at the discovery.

The seventh day dawned clear and cool, with the promise of heat to come quickly. Ian wanted to try an area that had a lot of kudu in it but he said it was very thick. That was a severe understatement. I have never seen a more thorn infested piece of bush in my life. Most impressive were what I assumed to be prickly pear cactus on steroids. Those things had bases that some oaks would be jealous of. I had worn my long pants over my shorts, and was glad that I did. We picked up a local gentleman by the name of Arthur, or as I like to call him, "Mr. Kudu." We began to drive into the mass of vegetation along trails, stopping periodically to glass the hillsides. One stop revealed the head and horns of a monster bull three hundred yards away. Ian told me that he had a broken tip just as I was trying to figure out how in the heck I'd ever get a shot at him.

Another stop revealed three bulls feeding together several hundred yards off. Two were nice, but young. The third had horns that curled parallel to each other to the point that they almost touched at each curl. He was certainly unique looking, but not what we were after. We saw several more bulls, but something always wasn't quite right, or we managed to spook them. Finally, Arthur suggested something very interesting. He took us to an old rickety platform, that reminded me of your typical whitetail tower blind. It overlooked a hillside and provided a great view over the hills and valleys. He explained that he and Pearce would in essence make a push toward us from a hillside about a mile away. The kudu naturally traveled the ridgeline we were on and maybe they could push something past us. Frankly, I was skeptical. There were miles and miles of bush that the kudu could melt into. In the thick cover, all they really had to do was the old whitetail trick of making a circle around the two of them.

Then, there was the platform itself. We actually had to climb up onto it. What's the big deal, you ask? I must say that the one nail on each rung going up fifteen feet in the air had me concerned. But not half as concerned as the broomstick size sticks that made the rungs. The platform was constructed in much the same manner. I climbed up after Ian, grabbing on to anything I could find with a death grip. When I settled in next to Ian, I could just envision a slow motion collapse of the platform into that mass of thorns below us. I did my best to breathe evenly so it wouldn't start swaying.

As I described at the beginning of this chapter, two bulls came busting out to us. Based on what I had seen, they looked good with each completing the required number of curls to be considered a mature bull. They were starting to get past us, and I was getting a little nervous when Ian said, "Take either one." Of course at that very moment they ducked into some impenetrable pocket of cover, so I pulled to the other side and waited. Finally I could see horns coming, but the brush was still too thick. At the very last moment one of them exposed himself just enough for me to send a hundred and eighty grains of Nosler partition on its way.

At the shot, they both scattered with the one I shot at coming right beneath the stand. I shot quickly as he ran past and he disappeared right back into the bush. He left a wake of moving tops, and then the brush stopped moving. I practically begged Ian to let me get down and check on him, but he wanted to wait for the guys so we could direct them to the spot and we could be ready for a follow up shot if necessary. After several minutes Arthur and Pearce tunneled by us and we directed them to the spot. Word drifted up from the dense brush that the bull was down.

The only problem at that point was that I'd have to actually move, in order to get down. The platform swayed more than was comfortable, but I made it to the ground in one piece. We started into the dark thorny nightmare, and I discovered why Ian wanted us to wait. After a slow anxious walk, we came upon the bull. I was speechless, this was the animal I wanted more than any other and he was lying at my feet.

The one animal the author wanted more than any other, a beautiful, mature bull kudu.

After admiring the bull for a while, I wondered how in the heck we could take any pictures in there. Ian said that we'd take him out to an opening. I had assumed that we'd quarter the bull on the spot in order to get him out, but Ian told me with a twinkle in his eye that we were going to carry him out. I wondered which "we" he was talking about. "We" cut some brush, covered the bull, and then headed back to the truck. We picked up some of Arthur's buddies with some kind of a stretcher. I knew there was no way they could thread their way out of there with a kudu on a stretcher and said as much. It soon became apparent that they knew exactly what they were doing. Several of the guys went back in to load the kudu, and a few of the others started chopping a trail back in there with machetes.

With a trail cut, they loaded up the bull, hoisted him on their shoulders and walked right out of there. We took several pictures and then headed back to butcher the bull. I told Ian that if I had gone home with just that one animal, the trip would have been worth it.

Carrying the kudu on the path that had been cut through the impenetrable bush.

With the kudu safely in the salt it was time to turn our attention to warthogs. The next steamy morning found us in an area known to carry some big tuskers. We tried every trick in the book over the next few days. We glassed, still hunted, sat on water holes and even stomped on some of their tunnels. All we saw were females, small males and several big kudu that seemed to know they were safe. As the sun set on the last day of my hunt, I marveled at where I was and what I had been lucky enough to experience over the past ten days. I also knew that one trip to Africa just wasn't enough, and I'd have to figure out a way to get back over there.

Chapter 20

Colorado Dream'n?
2002

I was breathing hard and my heart was pounding in my ears. The buck was huge, and he was in the brush just over a hundred yards up the hill. If he came through the same opening as the does, I'd have a shot. If he ventured just a few steps over the hill, he'd be gone for good. I was in the Front Range of the Colorado Rockies, once again hunting mulies with Golden Gate Outfitters.

I had arrived in the familiar surroundings and beautiful ranch house early, and spent much of the day before the season opener wandering the ranch, seeing many does and small bucks, along with a few very good animals. From what I could see, and based on my past experiences with the Golden Gate crew, it certainly appeared that I was in for a great week.

Opening day of the second season was cool and clear, a perfect day to go on a morning hike. I was being guided by Art Warren, an Engineer who spends his free time finding steep hills for his hunters to climb. Art is a good natured person who I've known for half a dozen years, and I've always enjoyed hunting with him. When it comes to big mule deer, he knows his stuff. We were accompanied for the morning by Art's brother Bob, who enjoys hunting as much as I do, and matches his brother's temperament. We ventured to a piece of land located off the main ranch dubbed the school house property. Unfortunately, I didn't pack any oxygen, and Art's idea of "down hill" somehow included portions of what I normally consider to be "up", but I guess Colorado natives would call "flat". Due to a summer of drought, and a lack of water on the property, we only saw a few does and some elk tracks.

We ventured back to the north end of the ranch in the afternoon and started walking up a hill next to an abandoned quarry. Glassing the surrounding area periodically as we progressed, Art suddenly pointed out a doe and small buck as they topped a hill about four hundred yards out. As we continued to glass, Art suddenly whispered, "Big buck." I think that's the first time I've heard Art say those words, so he immediately got my attention. The buck was indeed "Big", but I really wanted a better look, so Art retreated to the truck to pick up the spotting scope. As Art left, I studied the buck and tried to make up my mind. He was huge in body, and his rack was extremely high with fairly good forks, but only around 21-22" wide. During four mule deer hunts and one elk hunt with these guys, my sense of reason has been permanently ruined, so after studying the deer in the spotting scope and consulting with Art, I finally decided not to give him a go. Heavy fog then rolled in for a good part of the afternoon, severely limiting our visibility. When it finally rolled out late in the afternoon we saw a few good bucks, but no shooters.

The second day dawned exceptionally cold and windy. We set off for a very deep, steep drainage on the western side of the ranch and slowly worked our way from one end to the other. Evidently the deer liked the cold wind even less than we did, as we couldn't locate anything until we hit the end of the drainage. There we found a small buck chasing a few does around at about three hundred fifty yards. They spotted us and started up the hill, spooking a good buck that exploded out of the cover and ran flat out for about a quarter mile before stopping and allowing us a look. It was absolutely amazing watching him effortlessly run over such rugged, unforgiving terrain. It would have taken us an hour to negotiate the ground that he did in thirty seconds. Once again he was still not quite what I was looking for. It had warmed considerably during the morning, and our trip out of the drainage was more productive as we located two very respectable 4x4 bucks in the low twenties on the way out as well as a number of smaller bucks, but decided to pass. The afternoon provided pleasant weather as we searched the center of the ranch. We saw a number of smaller bucks, a huge bodied sumo wrestler of a buck with a relatively small rack and two very good 4x4's. Once again, the Golden Gate brain washing kicked in, and we didn't pursue either buck. We returned to camp, and found that one of the other hunters had taken a very nice 23"-24" 4x4. A perfect end to the day.

Day three was a beautiful day, clear, crisp and calm. We started at the eastern end of the ranch, where we drove to the end of a knob and walked to several good glassing locations. At the first stop, we saw a very good 22" 4x4 with deep forks, good mass and tall brow tines feeding in an open bowl about four hundred fifty yards away. Once again he wasn't quite the buck I was looking for, but he was very, very tempting. We made the rounds and returned to our original location, and the 4x4 was still there, working his way nearer to us. Art said, "Come on, I've got to get you out of here before that thing gets any closer." Starting back to the west we saw a nice young 4x5 with perhaps a 25" spread. We watched him for a while thrashing some brush and otherwise convincing himself that he was the biggest, baddest buck on the mountain. As we continued on, I noticed a 4x4 with good backs but crab claw fronts chasing some does around, about a hundred yards up on a wooded ridge. We were just ready to continue on when I noticed antlers flashing through the brush. "Hold it," I whispered, "There's another buck." Two sets of binoculars raised, and it was immediately apparent that he was one of those bucks that required no conferencing, discussion or other such foolishness. Art immediately said, "You need to take that buck," as I was fumbling for my rifle. I racked a shell into the chamber, and looked back up the hill for the buck. He had moved past our position down the ridge line, so we paralleled him for about thirty yards. Art never looked down, keeping the buck pegged in his glasses. I got into a sitting position, but the buck never presented a good shot through the brush. At Arts command to "C'mon" I stood and raced along the ridge for another seventy yards and once again settled into a sitting position. Art was whispering the buck's location, and said that he was coming out. There was some momentary confusion when the crab claw buck switched positions with the big boy, but we got it figured out as he stepped into an opening and the other deer cleared. I took a quick breath, held low on his chest and squeezed the trigger. The Browning Stainless Stalker, .300 Win Mag barked and the brush erupted with deer. With the impact of the recoil, I did not see what happened to the deer and asked Art where he went. He said that the deer disappeared at the shot, dropping in his tracks. We both started up the hill to see just how big this beast was. I got two thirds of the way up the hill and decided to run a quick search for oxygen molecules. As I stood there, sucking in the near vacuum, Art continued up the hill (Colorado natives have a third lung), turned to me and said, "I think you're going to like this one Glenn." Once the spots stopped dancing in front of my eyes, I continued up the hill, and couldn't believe my eyes when I got to the buck. He was an absolutely spectacular 5x6, with good mass, deep forks, and a 31" outside spread. To say that I was thrilled is a severe understatement.

This is what dreams are made of, a 31" 5x6 mulie on the ground.

Chapter 21
When Porcupines Attack

One of the overlooked benefits of a life in the outdoors are some of the amusing things that happen during a hunting or fishing trip. Here are a few that proved to be somewhat humorous.

Some of the most fun I've had in the woods is when I'm out turkey hunting. It's amazing that we even have turkeys in New York. They were quite abundant during the European colonization, but a combination of market/subsistence hunting and habitat destruction for farming basically eliminated the wild turkey from New York. With the expansion westward, much of the farmland was abandoned, allowing the land to revert back to forest and suitable turkey habitat. The only items that were missing were the turkeys. In the mid nineteen hundreds turkeys began to repopulate the southwestern portion of the state via an expanding population from Pennsylvania. In the nineteen fifties several thousand game farm turkeys were released throughout the state, but since they didn't have any wild instincts they did not survive. Starting in the late fifties the Department of Environmental Conservation started trapping and transplanting the birds that had established themselves in the southwestern part of the state. They continued the practice for about thirty-five years. The turkey's repopulated the state at an astonishing rate, and are now found virtually everywhere in huntable populations.

The end result of all this for me was that about the time I entered college there was a huntable population in the southern part of the state around my relative's land. I bought a box call, grabbed my trusty Remington 1100 and headed for the woods. That first predawn gobble had me hooked, and I've been hunting them ever since.

I woke up one spring morning at some ridiculous hour and I could hear a steady rain outside. I resisted the urge to shut off the alarm and go back to sleep, and headed out into the ink black morning. I heard nothing as dawn came and went, and after making a large slow circle, I decided to set up in a likely looking place and just call for a while. I set up my tree umbrella, thankfully crawled underneath and started calling. Almost immediately I got an answering gobble from about three hundred yards away. It was fairly early in my turkey hunting career and I had had some gobblers hang up on me. My solution was to close the distance to the turkey quickly after that first gobble. With this solution firmly imbedded in my mind, as soon as that bird gobbled, I sprinted from under the umbrella and ran toward the bird, intending to cut the distance in half before calling again.

    I was jogging around a small knoll, when I met the gobbler running full speed from the other direction. We both skidded to a stop about fifteen yards apart. He had the same surprised expression on his face as I had on mine and for a split second we just looked at each other. Then he decided he had an appointment elsewhere and took off in the opposite direction. I just laughed and shook my head, wondering if he was running toward my call or my umbrella.

    My sister married Steve Strife in 2001. Steve was quite a hunter and while we had different areas that we deer hunted, each spring we'd get together on the weekends and go turkey hunting. He had access to several pieces of property and I had a couple, so together we could cover some ground. The first morning we hunted together I went with him to a farm that had a combination of open fields and woods and was generally rolling hills. We walked up a steep ridge in the predawn darkness, that had me puffing like a steam locomotive and stopped at the top. The tweaty birds were first to begin to talk, then the crows started up which was always an indicator to me that it was "That time." Sure enough, a gobbler sounded off down the ridgeline about a hundred yards away, then another, and another. Pretty soon the whole ridge for about a half mile was just ringing with gobbles.

    We got set up about fifty yards apart and started calling. Soon the birds hit the ground and we had a gobbler working his way toward us through the woods. Steve later related seeing flashes of movement as the bird moved through with a few hens, just out of shooting range, gobbling his head off. Just as he moved through, another gobble sounded off just over the ridge behind me. We both rotated a hundred and eighty degrees and listened as the bird came up the hill, his booming gobbles vibrating the ground. He was just about to top the ridge when a hen clucked to my right. The Tom evidently saw her and she looked more attractive than I sounded. Pretty soon he was headed away from me, still gobbling.

All of a sudden a gobble sounded right behind me from Steve's location. A bird had been listening to the action and had snuck in from behind us. He picked out a spot about three feet behind Steve to make his entrance gobble. Steve levitated about three feet off the ground then turned to look around the tree. He found himself face to face with the bird. If turkeys could scream, this one would have. He turned and fled into the brush before Steve could make the shot. After those ten minutes of frantic action, the woods went silent. I walked over to Steve and asked him why he bothered to bring his gun if he was going to try to catch them by hand. I won't provide his reply....

Another cool spring morning found me in the woods pursuing Thanksgiving dinner. It was getting just light enough to see. I was easing along an old logging trail listening for a gobbler to sound off from the roost. I had not heard a bird, but I did hear some leaves crunching ahead and to the right of the trail. As I approached, a big porcupine wandered out into the middle of the trail. I decided to hurry him on his way and walked up to within about ten yards of him. He immediately flared into a defensive posture turning his back to me. I figured I'd get a little closer to push him off the trail. I kept easing nearer until I was about three yards from him, but he still would not move off. Then, he suddenly whirled and charged. After a split second of surprise, I started backpedaling and realized that he was actually gaining on me. I thought to myself, "Holy cow, I might have to actually shoot this thing!" I picked up the speed, hoping I wasn't going to trip over anything, while taking the shotgun off my shoulder. Luckily, the porcupine is much like a cheetah, in that it's got a relatively short burst of speed when pursuing its pray. Then it burns out and has to stop. Well, he hit his limit, and skidded to a halt. Then, with as much disdain as he could muster, he waddled off into the woods. I chuckle about that moment every time I think about it. I could also imagine the scene in the emergency room, "Honest Doc, I was mauled by a porcupine!"

My parents met the Shew family when I was fairly young. They got along well and soon life long friendships were formed. They've been more like family than friends ever since. Bob and Shelba are the old folks, and I do mean old, because they're my parent's age. Kelly, Mike and Robin are the kids, which are around the same age as my sister and me. When I was about fourteen, Bob, Mike, my father and I were frog hunting from johnboats on a little stream one day. We were using hollow point twenty two's and shooting the frogs in the head. We had shot a bunch of big frogs, and we were actually out of ammunition. I was in a boat with Bob, and we were on the way back to the trucks when we spotted a big frog just sitting in the open. Bob maneuvered the boat so I was close to the frog and I took an oar and slammed it down on the frog as hard as

I could. I was looking for the frog in the muck, when there was some kind of a noise from the stern of the boat. I turned and looked at Bob, who was covered from head to toe in what the frog used to be sitting in. It was the funniest thing I had ever seen in my life. I nearly fell overboard I was laughing so hard. Bob didn't seem to be quite as amused as I was for some reason ...

I was bow hunting on my Aunt and Uncle's property in the Finger Lakes of New York on a crisp sunny fall day. I was stationed about twenty feet up a tree in my trusty Baker climbing tree stand. I had been hunting for a couple of hours, and there had been a red squirrel below, busily doing whatever it is they do when they're not chattering at me. All of a sudden, an intruder boldly arrived on the scene. They immediately started chasing each other around, presumably arguing about nuts or something else just as important. They had been going at it for quite some time and I had become thoroughly entranced by the duel, forgetting about deer hunting entirely. They were racing up and down trees, going in circles, leaping from branch to branch, just tearing things up. One of them came racing up a tree about five feet in front of me, with his pursuer right behind. Just as he got to eye level he made a leap for a branch.... and missed. As the squirrel plummeted to the ground, I did too. My stomach just dropped like I was falling, and I actually grabbed hold of the stand with both hands. He hit the ground with a squirrel sized thump, and instead of lying there, he bounced right up and bounded away. I, on the other hand was sitting up in the tree trying to convince my body that I didn't just fall out of the tree with the squirrel.

One year when I was hunting with Randy Christensen we headed out the day before the season to do some glassing. Randy was driving his white SUV, which had become the color of the local dirt roads. We parked, grabbed our glasses and headed for a good vantage point. We spent a half hour glassing, seeing a few deer and decided to head for a different area.

We arrived back at the truck to find that a herd of cows had licked the side of the truck. This was of a course a great source of amusement, especially for some of the comments that could then be made. It was thought that perhaps this was a hint that the truck might need a good washing. A question was brought up concerning the kind of mileage a Cowlick got. Of course the biggest issue was the concern about the legality of baiting for cows.

Chapter 22
Fog, Wind and Trophy Dalls
2003

Reprinted from the Journal of Safari Big Game Hunting Magazine

I was still out of the big ram's sight, fifty yards shy of reaching the small ridge, and the rams three hundred yards to my left were getting nervous. As I watched, the larger of the two started easing up the hill. Swearing silently to myself, I decided to ignore those two, and double time it to the ridge. Breathing hard, I peaked over the edge and saw that the ram was alert and looking right at me. A quick range reading put him at two hundred thirty five yards. I flipped down the bipod and pushed my Browning Stainless Stalker up onto the ridge.

Alaska! After years of dreaming of going on a sheep hunt, at last it was time to put the weeks of biking and mountain climbing to the test. My flights from northern NY to Fairbanks were long but uneventful. After a night's stay there, I continued on to outfitter Richard Guthrie's base camp near Galbraith Lake on the northern slope of the Brooks Range, with four other hunters. It was a great flight, with clear skies allowing us to take in the vast unspoiled wilderness. Rich shuttled people to their spike camps throughout the afternoon in his Super Cub. I was one of the last ones out for the day and Rich took me to a beautiful big valley with a river meandering down the middle and high peaks and drainages adjoining from either side. I was greeted by guide Terry Boyle and a squadron of thankful mosquitoes saying grace. Terry is just what you would expect to find in a good Alaskan guide. He's been in Alaska for over twenty years, obviously has a lot of outdoor savvy and he's a nice guy to boot. Among some of his endeavors, he's a professional photographer, heavy equipment operator, professional fisherman and an ex world champion log roller. Just for fun he breaks trail for the Iditarod, and takes several hundred mile snowmobile trips. He's currently involved with some outdoor videography work throughout Alaska.

The next day was sunny, warm and clear. Since it was the day before sheep season opened, we went on a scouting trip sticking to the main valley, and glassing the drainages. We found a potential shooter ram up one of the drainages a few miles away, and decided to try that in the morning.

Opening day dawned clear and warm. We walked the mile or so north to the drainage, crossed the river and dropped our hip boots on the other side. Our "sentry ram" a half curl ram we were to see in the same location almost every day, was stationed at the head of the drainage. Terry said he was giving tail signals about us to the other sheep in the area. I successfully resisted the urge to shoot his tail off and continued on. We started up the drainage heading east, and noticed tracks of a grizzly and a wolf in the streambed. A mundane sight for the average Alaskan, but it was a small thrill for me. You just don't get to see that kind of thing in upstate NY. After a mile or so the drainage turned generally back to the south. During one of our glassing sessions, I spotted a band of five rams a few miles up the drainage. After studying them in the spotting scope, it appeared that possibly one or two were full curl, but we needed to get closer to be sure. As we continued on Terry suddenly noticed a ram running up a mountain behind us by a mile and a half. He disappeared behind a rock outcrop, as another ram started up the slope. We looked the second ram over, and decided that he wasn't quite full curl and the first ram never reappeared. As we continued up the drainage, the five rams evidently thought we were up to no good, as they also disappeared over the wrong side of the mountain. It appeared that the drainage we were following was roughly paralleling the main valley, and it looked like it eventually swung back around to the west. To make a long story short, it didn't, and we ended up having to walk up to the snow line over a pass and still had two and a half miles to get to the valley floor. Our best route down was a steep snow chute, an experience I won't soon forget as I spent most of my time trying not to become a toboggan. Half way down the snow chute, Terry suddenly froze. Two rams were feeding close to our elevation about four hundred yards away. A quick evaluation revealed that they weren't shooters, so we continued down the drainage. It's hard to explain how nasty that terrain can be. A lot of the mountains contain a jumble of rocks from about six inches to four feet thrown together in tremendous rockslides. Most of the walking seems to involve stepping from one unstable rock to another in almost a controlled fall. It's very treacherous going down steep inclines where your feet can be out from under you in a heartbeat. Shortly thereafter, rain and fog came rolling down the valley like a blanket. Once we finally hit the river, we just waded across the thigh high snow melt since our hip boots were two miles up the valley. We sloshed back to camp, arriving just before 1 am. That was my introduction to sheep hunting. I was pretty tired, but I could have sworn I heard Terry mention something about it being a good warm up for the days to follow.

The next morning the rain and fog that had developed the previous night remained, the mountains were completely covered, so we slept in. There wasn't much we could do so we stayed in camp all day. Terry introduced me to "spam-cakes", a pancake baked around a slab of spam. I really think he's been doing a little too much cold weather camping without a hat. The local mosquitoes were now full and storing provisions for the winter. Late in the day Terry stood at the tent opening and said that unless the tundra was growing trees, there was a herd of caribou down the valley. That got my attention, because I also had a caribou tag, but there were no big bulls in the group.

Heavy fog blanketed the mountains for a good portion of the hunt.

Dawn of the third day came and went, it was still foggy with a steady rain and the river was raging. We glassed a few caribou, but decided that they weren't worth trying to cross the river for. I thought I saw a bull over there trying on our hip boots. The temperature began to drop and the mosquitoes finally left us alone. For supper, I was introduced to another of Terry's specialties, mooseghetti. I wasn't sure which part of the moose was involved, and decided not to ask.

The forth morning looked promising, so we walked a mile to the south and watched in disbelief as the fog rolled back in. We headed back to be "cot potatoes" for a while. To keep me in shape, Terry suggested a climb up to a small basin above camp. We got up there and found nothing, but it did feel good to be doing something. The fog teased us on and off the rest of the day. Late in the day, we actually could have hunted the east side of the river, but it looked like we should be surfing it, not crossing it.

I awoke on the fifth day of the hunt, and I stared at the ceiling of the tent. We had really only hunted one day so far and I was starting to get nervous. I couldn't imagine the years of planning and thousands of miles of travel all coming down to looking at the inside of a tent. Luckily the rain had stopped and the fog had lifted. The river had dropped a bit, so Terry taped up his boots and a pair of rubber pants and managed to wade across to pick up our hip boots. The river was still very high, and it looked like more weather was brewing to the south, so we elected to stay on the west side of the river. About three miles from camp, at one pm, Terry suddenly stopped and said he saw some sheep at the top of a drainage. I looked up to where he was indicating and saw some tiny white specks just inside the stratosphere. Through the spotting scope we could see slightly bigger white specks. We picked out four rams, of which it appeared that one or two were probably shooters. The only approach would be to walk across the entrance of the drainage and up the back side of the ridge. We were about a mile and a half from the sheep, so we didn't think we'd spook them walking across in plain sight. We safely got to the other side and found some of the worst terrain I had seen yet. It was about as steep as I'd ever want to climb without a rope or helicopter, and much of the slope was very unstable. We trudged our way up the mountain for several hours, till we hit a precipice about seven hundred yards from the rams that we just couldn't work our way around. We discussed our options, and decided that the only way we could proceed was to briefly walk up on the ridge, exposing ourselves to the sheep. In the "hunker" position, we slowly eased up the ridge, and then back out of sight. Neither of us dared to show our faces, so we weren't sure if we pulled it off or not. Another hundred and fifty yards and we were truly stuck. We were out of ground, and would be totally exposed in any move we made.

This picture was taken during the stalk, which began on the valley floor below.

    Three of the rams were visible, and Terry pronounced the one straight up the slope to be a very good ram of 38", with the two to our left being a small ram and a borderline legal ram. The forth ram was nowhere to be found. We ate lunch and discussed the situation. We came up with only one alternative. I'd put on a white overcoat, play sheep and try to approach as closely as possible while Terry filmed the action from our current location. Feeling very conspicuous and a little silly, I eased over the ridge and started toward the ram. The first couple hundred yards were fairly uneventful with all three rams occasionally glancing in my direction, but pretty much ignoring me. I reached a flat grassed outcropping and stopped to catch my breath and take a quick range reading. The ram was three hundred fifty yards away, feeding with his back to me. The winds were gusting over thirty mph, so there was no way I could shoot from there, but I was beginning to feel like I could probably pull the stalk off. I racked a shell into the chamber, clicked the safety on, took a deep breath, and continued on. There was a depression just ahead of me leading to a small ridge-line that would keep me out of sight from the big ram. I reached the depression without alerting the ram and breathed a sigh of relief. After reaching the ridge as described earlier, I quickly scampered up the five foot vertical rock face, and settled into a prone position. I took a few quick breaths, aimed eight inches to the left of the lungs for the wind, squeezed the trigger and the .300 Win Mag barked. By the time I recovered from the recoil, the ram had already dropped and was beginning to tumble down the slope. Luckily he only rolled about 30 yards before he was stopped by a large rock. It was six thirty pm.

The author with a great dall ram, following almost 4000 vertical feet of climbing.

Terry packed up his video equipment, and started walking up to meet me with my pack, his pack and his rifle. An agreeable arrangement that I wish I had thought of earlier. I spent a few minutes hyperventilating on the ridge, and then started back down to meet him. After mutual congratulations we continued up to the ram. When I started on this adventure, any legal ram would have been fantastic. As we approached, I was amazed at what a dream ram he really was with horns sweeping around past full curl and tipping out. I couldn't have been happier, even after Terry mentioned the work ahead of us to get him out. Before we touched the ram, Terry, with some native blood, followed his ancestor's traditions honoring the ram by making a tobacco offering in four directions to the creator.

After taking some video and pictures, we deboned the meat, cut the head off at the neck to be caped back at camp, transferred some of Terry's gear to my pack, placed the meat in his pack and the head in mine. I did some of my training with a forty pound pack, and guessed that my pack was somewhere in that neighborhood. Terry's pack must have been ninety pounds or better.

We found a little better route down than we came up, but it was still perilous. We left the top of the mountain at about ten pm. We had gone perhaps two hundred yards when Terry's feet went out from under him, and his top half tried to pass his bottom half. Luckily his rifle was dragging along under him and slowed his decent to the point that he could regain his footing. This was a grim reminder of how serious the situation could quickly become. We had progressed about three quarters of the way down the mountain by twelve thirty am. We were both tired from the climb, the light wasn't very good and the footing was still bad, so we decided to drop our packs and head back to camp. We got back to the tents at about two forty five am, got some soup, water and juice into our stomachs and went to sleep. At about five thirty AM our camp was invaded by a hunter and guide from the next valley over. They had shot a sheep about the same time as me, and decided that it was closer and less dangerous to proceed to our camp. They had been walking all night and were exhausted. We got them settled into our tents and everyone dropped back off to sleep. A bit of excitement ensued in mid morning as a pair of musk ox walked within a few hundred yards of camp prompting a flurry of snapping shutters. We left shortly thereafter and returned about six hours later with the sheep. Rich flew in a bit after we got back, and established that the ram was twelve and a half years old, and Terry was right on the money at 38". Close rings on his horns for several years indicated just how tough life was for an old ram in that extreme environment. We also took a few minutes to look at the topo map, and it showed that we had made nearly a four thousand foot ascent to get to the rams. I'm glad I didn't know that before we started up the mountain.

The following day we slept in, then finished caping, fleshing and salting the cape. We had a rare treat, as a wolverine loped down the mountain near camp. Several groups of caribou also moved through early. A group of about fifty ran by camp, with one or two shooters in the group, but no chance for a shot. I glassed a pair of caribou breaking over the hill about a half mile to the north, but something about them didn't look quite right. Then it struck me that I was looking at wolves, and probably the reason for the unsettled movements of the caribou. The wolves were directly down wind, and probably winded us and headed for the hills, because we never saw them again. Another storm was brewing in the afternoon, and the caribou movement slackened. The hard rain began mid afternoon and continued through the night.

The final day of the hunt arrived and a cold wind was blowing down the valley from the north, accompanied by rain and fog. I awoke early, and took a walk around the valley looking for caribou and then returned to camp after seeing just a few animals. Shortly after lunch, a herd of about fifty animals was seen coming from the south. Recognizing a few of the individuals, it was apparently the same group that had come running from the north the previous day. Terry and I picked out three good bulls in the group, and settled on trying for a wide bull first. My first shot was just shy of three hundred yards, and between the wind and the caribou's movement, I caught him a bit far back and a finishing shot was required. We spent the next few hours packing the meat to the "airstrip". I was supposed to fly out that evening, but bad weather precluded that from happening. The next morning, the fog was just sitting on the deck and I figured I was going to be there a while. In fact, from the looks of things, probably through winter. But, in the afternoon the fog broke and Rich managed to come in and get me back to base camp in time for the flight back to Fairbanks. Simply put, it was a great adventure. I wonder if there's a moose with my name on it up there somewhere? I guess there's one way to find out.

A bonus during the sheep hunt was this wide caribou in velvet.

Chapter 23
Inyati on the Run
2004

Reprinted from the Journal of Safari Big Game Hunting Magazine

Wayne quickly got me on the sticks and tried to see how good the bedded bull was. Eventually easing about five yards to my left, he finally gave the thumbs up and whispered "Shoot him when he stands." The tsetses were arguing over my more tender parts and the mopane flies swarmed unmolested about my head as time stood still and my whole world revolved around that dark lump in the brush. I don't know how many years I stood there, my heart hammering in my ears, when I suddenly sensed a change in the wind direction. "Here we go," I said to myself as I sighted through the dusty scope at a spot about a foot above the buffalo's back. What happened next is impossible to describe. Instead of standing to see what was going on, the bull caught our scent and literally launched himself off the ground into a full run in a heartbeat. It happened so fast it was just a blur of motion. I was stunned, there's no way anything that big can be that fast. Wayne brought me back to reality with, "Come on, they're running," and we took off on our daily wind sprints.

I was hunting Cape Buffalo in the thick jess of northern Zimbabwe, a life long dream come true. I had booked my hunt with HHK Safaris through Collins Kellogg Sr., practically a neighbor of mine in upstate New York. My Professional Hunter was Zimbabwean, Wayne Williamson, accompanied by trackers Cornelius (Connie) and Lovemore. Wayne's one of those guys you hope to get as a PH. He's knowledgeable, has a good sense of humor, works incredibly hard and most importantly he's very familiar with the critters that can bite back. In short, he's a professional in every sense of the word. Following a stay at the Victoria Falls Safari Lodge and a photo safari at the Chobe National Game Park in Botswana, we flew to the Omay region south of

Lake Kariba. My first impression upon landing at the short airstrip was thick bush and the very embodiment of "tall grass". Of course I've read about the tall grass, but only seeing it in person can do it justice. It generally ranged from wisps a few feet high to a tawny thatch work well over my head, able to hide an elephant with ease. Then add in a tangled mass of trees, brush and scrub and arm everything with various sized thorns and you've got Inyati country in northern Zimbabwe.

I had some non hunting days to burn, so we spent the first day setting some leopard baits for fellow hunter Dave Miller, who's PH was delayed by a wounded vehicle (just a flesh wound). The next day, it was time to get serious. Early in the morning, looking down on a drainage from a high cliff, Wayne located a large herd below, working its way up from the water. We drove as close as we could, I loaded my .375 Browning Stainless Stalker, set the Leupold 1-4x on one, took a deep breath (or two) and started out on my first buffalo hunt. We walked quickly for about a half-mile before we got to within about a hundred yards of the herd. After the fickle wind busted us a couple of times, we eventually made a complete circle around the herd as the wind steadied and ended up directly in front of them. Wayne glassed the animals we could see and whispered that a good bull was coming right at us. I was on the sticks, safety off, waiting for the bull to clear the brush. Minutes later, with my legs turning to rubber, the bull stepped clear at about twenty five yards. Wayne said he wanted one clear frontal view of the boss before I dropped the hammer. The bull eventually turned, and Wayne whispered "Don't shoot, he's too young." He continued to glass the other animals, but no mature bulls materialized. Eventually, the herd became aware of our presence and trotted off. Wayne later explained that the bull needed a year or so to grow a really solid boss. He also said that he almost had me shoot anyway, since the bull was very good, and the setup was perfect. He then added that it rarely works that way. Several hot, thorn torn days to follow made me realize just how right he was.

First thing the next morning a large herd literally ran across the road in front of us. Not believing our good fortune we alternately snuck, walked, cursed and ran with that herd for about a mile, but it became obvious that they weren't going to slow down until they hit Zambia. Then we made a short stalk on a small herd in a drainage, but there were no shooters. Later in the morning we went to the Ume River, cut some salad plate size tracks heading into the jess and followed for a while until we determined from the forage that they were actually a day old. I say, "we determined" because when Wayne told me, I'm pretty sure I nodded my head in the affirmative and grunted. We crossed to the other side of the river, and picked up the spoor of a small herd of six to eight animals with a few big tracks. We had been following for a short while when Wayne pointed to the ground and said "One of these buffalo is bleeding." Being one for making profound statements in the face of adversity, I muttered "Great," and we continued on. So we had the added bonus of knowing that one of the buffalo that we would likely find at "tag, you're it" distance might not have much of a sense of humor. Great.

Above a monster croc sun bathes on the Chobe River and below, a nice bull buffalo stepped out of the tall grass for a stare down. This is why solid bullets are made.

We eventually caught up to the group in the heavy cover after another hour's tracking, but there were no old bulls in the group. It appeared that the likely source of the blood was a cow with a damaged horn. After we left them, we found another big herd and tried a stalk that involved making believe I was a snake and ensuring that my entire body blended in with the native soils, to no avail. Lunchtime involved a very brief but enthusiastic elephant charge on the truck that neither Wayne nor I saw. However the guys in the back evidently had a good look from the racket they were making. While not being familiar with the language, I believe the call to abandon ship was almost given. We tried the herd later, and swirling winds busted us again.

This cow elephant was part of a small herd. She was trying to make up her mind whether to charge or amble off into the dense underbrush.

Dr. Gary Robbins, another hunter in camp had turned down a few very good bulls the previous day, looking for a very big, old, and especially ugly dugga boy. Wayne looked at some footage of the bulls and was impressed enough to suggest that we have a go at them. Following several hours of tracking, we found the herd in heavy brush. That heavy brush resulted in Wayne and me looking at two different bulls, busting them out of there at halitosis range and enough running to qualify for a marathon. They ended up on a steep ridge line and waited on top for our approach and then crashed out of there as we reached the summit. We stayed on them for the rest of the day with no luck.

At the end of the day, on the way back to camp we ran across some waterbuck, and after a stalk and a sprint up a hill I made a good shot on a nice twenty seven inch bull as he was sneaking away on an adjacent hill.

This waterbuck was a nice bonus one afternoon as the party was returning to camp.

On the fourth day, we didn't find any fresh spoor until about nine thirty am when we started tracking a large herd out of the river. We were just out of the river bottom when a low ominous rumble resounded just twenty yards to our right. I, like Connie immediately thought, "Buffalo," but somewhere amidst the next three or four grunts Wayne said quietly "Lion." Thinking that I was too young to be eaten, I had my rifle up and ready for a full frontal assault in a flash. Wayne, practically stifling a yawn, gazed through his binoculars into the tall golden grass looking for the cat. Presumably to determine if he could take it by hand or perhaps require a weapon of some sort such as a pointy stick should the lion decide to get up close and personal. He explained as we backed off that normally lions would run away, unless they're on a kill. If we had not walked away, we probably would have been treated to a mock charge, complete with growling, roaring, and flashing teeth. Great. Making a detour around the lion, we tracked the herd for about two hours until we bumped them. The wind was acting up again, so we decided to leave them until the afternoon when the wind should steady. We got back on the herd shortly before four pm. With a good steady breeze, we worked them for the rest of the afternoon. We'd make an approach, glass the animals we could see, back off, circle, and make another approach. Finally Wayne decided that there were no shooters in the group, just a huge bodied young bull that was going to be massive in a few years.

Gary once again had found some good bulls that were not quite ugly enough to shoot the previous day. So, shortly after six am in the chilly morning, we were on the spoor of the three bulls Gary had left the previous evening. Three hours of tracking through the thick thorn infested scrub had removed the chill from the air and the sun was starting to make its presence known. The tracks led from a relatively open area to an especially thick portion of the jess. It wasn't quite "crawl on your belly" thick, but thick enough to lose the end of your gun barrel every once in a while. Looking at the tangle, a seasoned veteran armed with a full four days worth of buffalo hunting experience, I just knew they were in there. Wayne stopped and had me change my opening salvo from a Nosler partition to a solid. He didn't have to explain why. I made sure my scope was set on one, and wished they made a smaller setting. Wondering if we should notify my next of kin, my rifle at port arms, thumb on the safety, senses on full alert, I slipped into the shadows. We drifted from one patch of impenetrable brush to the next, playing some kind of high stakes hide and seek with something exceedingly big that might be very displeased at being found.

The morning chill was just a fading memory. The sun was unrelenting and the heat seemed to emerge from everywhere. Even the breeze was like a furnace. Unbelievably, another two and a half hours had passed. The world had become a very simple place for me. Just place one step in front of the next as quietly as possible, scan up ahead while Connie did the hard work. Suddenly Wayne froze, breaking me out of my reverie. "They're right there," he whispered, trading the rifle for the sticks from Connie. We crawled forward for perhaps fifteen yards, when Wayne stopped again. I was behind some brush and couldn't see the bulls and was in the process of moving to Wayne's side, when he said "One of them just stood up." Evidently, the bull had heard us or seen movement and decided to investigate. Just as I got into position, the bull walked into the clear at about fifteen yards and with no hesitation broke into a run, taking the other bulls with him. Wayne sprinted after the bulls with me right behind. After about a hundred yards it was apparent that they weren't going to slow or turn so we gave up the pursuit. As I sat down in the shade all I could think is that we just needed three more seconds with that bull. One second for Wayne to say "Take him," and two more for me to get the shot off. Five and a half hours of tracking, and who knows how many miles, and we couldn't catch a break.

Following standard procedure we sat and sweated in the meager shade for about forty minutes, and then with few words we were back on the spoor again. We followed quickly until the running tracks became walking tracks and resumed the same familiar routine. Perhaps a half hour had passed when Wayne stopped quickly, put his glasses up and indicated that we were right on top of them. Fifteen yards away, looking much like the surrounding shadows, the back of a bedded buffalo could just be made out. As described at the beginning of the story, they busted out of there and we followed with all due haste. We ran a hundred yards and stopped to listen. Once we determined where they were headed, we were on the run again. Another hundred yards and my legs were starting to feel the morning's hike. The buffalo were headed toward the same ridgeline the earlier group had used to give us the slip. Wayne knew that it opened up a bit and hoped to catch the bulls as they went up the side, so we ran some more. My breath came in gasps and my heart pounded in my ears as we broke into the relative open area at the base of the ridge. Directly in front of us at about a hundred yards, walking quickly along the base of the ridge were eight bull buffalo. Why eight when we were following three, I have no idea. Perhaps they requested reinforcements. Wayne immediately threw up the sticks for me and put his glasses to work. I could tell with my naked eye that the lead bull was huge, much bigger in body than any of the others. Wayne took about a half second to reach the same conclusion, glanced at the massive boss on the bull and told me to bust it. I had one opening in front of the bull, and when he touched the cross hares the .375 kicked in my hands, and a three hundred grain Federal Premium Sledgehammer was on its way. The bull bucked and started angling up the hill even as the bullet's impact resounded in my ears. "Hit him again!" Wayne yelled. Just as I was about to squeeze the trigger, the other bulls ran in front of him and I pulled off until they cleared. As the last bull ran by, the big bull stumbled, fell to the ground, and started to roll down the ridge. For some reason I took my eye off the bull as he rolled. I don't know whether I was moving for a better angle, getting the sticks reset or checking my shoelaces, but when I looked back up all I could see was dust. According to Wayne the bull had stopped rolling. "He's just below the red rock, hit him again," Wayne said, and we went back and forth about where I was supposed to be shooting. Finally

I just aimed below the red rock and dropped the hammer. "You just shot the rock," Wayne said, and although it was obvious to me that I had in fact shot under the rock as instructed, I didn't figure it was the right time to defend my shooting ability. Wayne indicated that he was about ten yards further down the hill, and I saw a lump of dark gray I had previously thought to be too big to be a buffalo, but it was. I shot him again, with no apparent objection. Wayne, a person who likes to keep his skin intact, and the experience to know what kind of fire power black death can withstand had us go up the ridge and place another shot into the bull's neck, again with no movement. Following a careful approach, there were congratulations all around. A boyhood dream had been fulfilled, and I couldn't have been happier.

Following five tough days of hunting, this big old bull hit the ground. Author is on the left, PH Wayne Williamson is on the right.

My first shot had taken out one shoulder, progressed through the center of the heart and had lodged in the far shoulder. The bull had been dead on his feet. Wayne said that he felt that this bull was one of the very few that might truly approach a ton in weight. Lacking my bathroom scales, I took his word for it. All I know is that he was absolutely massive. He had honest fifteen inch bosses and was thirty-eight inches wide with the deep thick worn horns of a mature bull. In retrospect, I'm glad we didn't take that bull on the first day, it would have been too easy.

Chapter 24
More Running in Zimbabwe
2004

During the afternoon after shooting the buffalo, we hunted close to camp along a riverbed, mainly for bushbuck, and walked right into a small herd of buffalo. Luckily there were no big bulls in the group, so I didn't feel too bad about how easily we had walked into them. We saw a few impala, but no bushbucks, so we headed back to camp for supper and some more planning. Wayne suggested heading to another area after a few more days, since several of the animals I was after were nonexistent, or rare in the area.

On the sixth day of the hunt, the welcome cool morning found us above a riverbed walking the drainage. We stopped in one spot to glass and I separated myself from the others to get a little different angle. After a few moments, I could hear something in the leaves a hundred yards below us. I motioned to Wayne that there was something down there, but he couldn't see it either. Finally I could make out movement and saw a bush pig routing around the leaves. As we moved out of the area, we spooked the pig and pretty soon there were several running across the riverbed. Wayne looked at the last one and said that if I ever wanted a bush pig, the last one was a big male. I foolishly said no, and we headed to another vantage spot. We walked for a few miles and saw some kudu cows and impala, but nothing worth dropping the hammer on.

Later on, we walked up a drainage that had some thick brush, hoping to run into a bushbuck. At one point we were walking through some thick grass, well over our heads when an animal erupted from in front of us. Wayne snapped his gun up, I stepped a bit to his left and did the same. This is exactly why hunting in Zimbabwe is so exciting, you never know when that noise in the bush is a buffalo or lion who's decided he doesn't like the color of your hat and is coming to adjust it off your head. In this case, it ended up being a bushbuck busting out of the cover, but you always have to be prepared for the worse. A few days earlier, a family of warthogs had just about put me into cardiac arrest doing the same thing.

We walked for a while down the drainage and then climbed out. I thought that we certainly were doing an awful lot of climbing in "flat" Africa, and there had better be a sheep at the top. There wasn't, but seeing the truck up there was close enough. That evening we found a different part of the drainage and glassed for bushbucks below. We didn't see any bushbucks but there must have been fifty elephants feeding down there. I must admit to watching the elephants a little too much for the remainder of the day, and soon the sun was disappearing behind the hillside and it was time to head back.

The next morning, Wayne suggested that we pack up and head for the Lemco Safari area in south central Zimbabwe a day earlier than planned. So we threw everything into the truck and started down the dusty bumpy roads headed south. It was a great way to see Zimbabwe, and I thoroughly enjoyed the trip. We stopped briefly in Bulawayo and I met Wayne's wife Muffy, who was very nice. We pulled into Lemco late in the day, and got settled in to our nice bungalows along the Bubi River (yes, it's pronounce the way you think) and began making plans for the following day.

The "river" that time of year was mostly sand, with a few water holes located periodically along the riverbed. We started our eighth day by picking up a local guide and then struck off in search of game. The area was loaded with animals, including the cats, elephants, and buffalo. There was even a crocodile sunning himself by one of the pools of water we came across. We saw a variety of game and made several stalks on herds of impala, which were everywhere. Wayne and I decided that with the abundance of impala and three days of hunting left, we'd hold out for a truly exceptional ram. Each stalk resulted in either spooked impala, or finding nothing large enough. We also saw a few kudu, each one making my heart beat a little faster, but there were no big bulls.

Late in the morning we were driving along when Wayne spotted a few blue wildebeest just off the trail. We drove past the animals and then walked back, slowly scanning the brushy terrain. Suddenly Wayne froze, and I followed suit. There were a few bulls directly in front of us at just under a hundred yards. Wayne sized them up, set the sticks for me and told me to shoot the one facing us. He was obviously getting nervous with the movement, so as soon as the crosshairs settled on his chest I squeezed the trigger. At the shot, he jumped sideways and took off to our right at a dead run. Wayne, who apparently enjoys running after more game than just buffalo, took off hot on his trail with me following on his heels. He slowed when the animal disappeared and began to track the blood trail. He turned and asked how I felt about the shot. I told him that the crosshairs had drifted a few inches to the left as the gun discharged, but it should still be good. After a few more minutes Wayne pointed to a dark spot in the brush a hundred yards out. The bull was down, but his head was still up. We decided to try a shot, but the brush deflected it. Since the bull remained down at the shot, we didn't think he was going anywhere so we circled for a better angle and I put a finishing shot through the lungs. As we inspected the great bull, we found that my first shot was just off center as I indicated, but still punched through the heart/lung area. They're just tough critters.

Author with a nice blue wildebeest.

Following pictures and loading the bull on to the truck, we headed back to camp and rested for a few hours during the heat of the day. As the sun started its downward turn, we were back on the trail to see what we could see. We were a very short distance from camp when Connie said something to Wayne and we stopped. As Connie and Wayne were busy chatting between themselves in some sort of foreign language, I looked up on the hillside in the general direction they were looking. I couldn't for the life of me see anything alive up there. For all I knew they were talking about an especially attractive tree, or cloud formation. Wayne turned to me and said, "Get out and take him." I responded with, "Okay, take what?" "Sorry, there's a warthog just to the side of us in the brush," he responded. I was on the wrong side of the truck, and it was blocking my view into the brush, so I baled out and eased around the side. Sure enough, there was a tusker forty yards out in the bush. I shifted my position to find an opening and squeezed off a round.

After coming up empty in South Africa previously, this nice warthog was taken.

The pig dropped at the shot, and I finally had the warthog that had eluded me for so long in South Africa. I was ecstatic. Then he launched himself to his feet and ran straight ahead, and directly into a tree. He dropped for a second time, disappearing in the grass, just as I was bearing down on him. I had just taken the rifle off my shoulder when he got up again and bolted for cover. We started tracking him, and pretty soon came upon him lying on his side. It was obvious that he was punched through both lungs, but he was still alive so I put a finishing shot in him. He was a great pig, with long thick tusks and I couldn't have been happier.

With the rest of the day left to us, we quickly dropped the pig off at the skinning shack and headed back out. My main objective at this point was kudu. There were a lot of them around, and I dearly loved hunting them. We spent a very enjoyable afternoon looking over a variety of game, but no large kudu or impala were seen. Back at camp, reports were circulating about an especially large black maned lion that had taken down a full grown giraffe all by himself. I had seen a bunch of giraffes on the trip and couldn't imagine a cat big enough or powerful enough to bring one down. Several good animals were taken by the other hunters in camp, and a group of us went to the skinning shack to take a look. As we walked back from the shack the three hundred yards to the camp in the dark, the thought of that lion would not leave my head. If he could bring down a giraffe, what sort of a challenge would an unarmed human be.... not much, huh. Although at that point at least he should have been full, and resting.

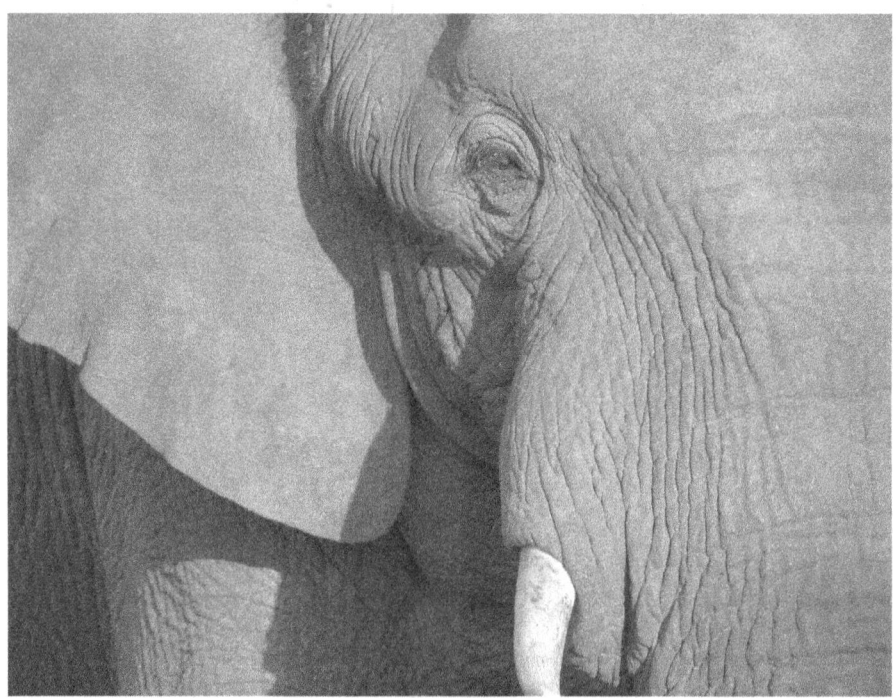

A nice bull elephant up close and personal. He wasn't a problem, but the cow and calf behind him had everyone's attention.

A chilly morning greeted us on the ninth day, but I knew from experience that as soon as the sun started to make its ascent, it would warm up in a matter of minutes. We started looking in the thick bush along the river for kudu. It was the next to last day of my hunt and it was time to find a big boy. After seeing several young bulls and cows, we found him. Actually we found him and a couple of his buddies. We were riding along the trail when Wayne brought us to a stop. I saw three bulls in the shadows, and Wayne quickly told me to take the middle one.

I never got the chance. They whirled away and headed down into the riverbed. We followed them down over the bank for a bit, then backtracked and made a large circle out in front of them. We dropped into the hot sand of the riverbed and began to ease our way along the thick foliage, periodically glassing ahead. Suddenly, ahead of us, kudu bulls burst out of the cover and sped across the sand. Wayne dropped the sticks in front of me and told me to hit the first one. I lined up the crosshairs and shot, just as Wayne said, "No wait shoot the last one," as another bull broke cover. He quickly confirmed a miss with Connie and me on the first bull and I lined up on the last one. Two more shots and I was standing with an empty gun and an open river in front of me. I couldn't believe that I had missed. I don't do much shooting at running game, but the sight picture looked good for two out of three of the shots.

As we slogged through the deep sand to check for a hit, I immediately realized what happened. The size of the kudu and the open ground had me estimating the distance at much less than the two hundred fifty to three hundred yards we covered. I'm sure I shot every one of those kudu exactly where they were about a half second after they left. I'm not sure that makes sense, but it sounds better than "I missed." Oh well, another tough lesson learned. I told Wayne to kindly provide a standing broadside shot next time and at least a minute for me to take a range reading, fill some sand bags and test the wind. He promised, and we continued on our way. We saw a few youngsters during the rest of the morning and returned to camp to wait out the mid day heat. We headed to a new area in the afternoon, and while we saw a good variety of game, we only saw three small kudu bulls, and a few good impala that wouldn't stand still for the required minute. On the way back to camp we came across a pack of wild dogs, a very rare sight in Africa these days. They were much bigger animals that I thought they'd be, and their patchwork of colors afforded them perfect camouflage. A few of the dogs stood on their hind legs to get a better look at us and then melted into the brush. My only disappointment was that it was a little too dark for pictures.

The last day of my hunt dawned and I marveled that the time had passed so quickly. We were heading down the side of the river and Wayne spotted a herd of impala. He pronounced one of the rams to be a shooter and I quickly got into position for the shot. The ram bolted at the shot and disappeared over a hill. A few moments later, Connie was on the blood trail and we came upon one of the most handsome and recognizable antelope in Africa. He was a very nice ram with good bases and a good shape to his horns. We loaded him in the truck, and became strictly kudu hunters.

There were many impala in the concession, this is a good representative of the quality.

We continued on our way, for perhaps an hour, when Wayne suddenly spotted a good bull kudu feeding in a small clearing a hundred and fifty yards off the road. He told Lovemore to continue driving for several hundred yards and then we dove off the truck and headed back. The difference in elevation between the back of the truck and eye level became painfully apparent. The thick brush loomed over our heads as we located the general area where he spotted the bull. We headed slowly into the bush, scanning as far into the shadows as we could. Several minutes passed when Wayne spotted movement forty yards ahead. A few steps more and the various animal parts added up to a bull kudu. Wayne shifted back and forth trying to make out the horns through the brush, and finally said,

"Fifty one." I took that to mean, "shoot" and asked him as much. He gave me the green light, so it was my turn to do the shifting back and forth. The first two holes I tried to look through didn't give me a shot, but the third one from bent knee exposed his chest. He just caught on to the movement as I squeezed the trigger.

This great kudu was taken during the waning moments of the hunt.

At the shot, the bull reared up on his hind legs and then bolted for cover. Wayne bolted right after him. Having been hunting with Wayne for a while I was ready, and had my track shoes tightly laced. We raced through the brush for a short distance and found the bull piled up. A finishing shot later, and I was looking at a magnificent majestic kudu bull. It was a great way to wrap up an adventure. The bull was huge, being bigger in both body and horn, and possessing a darker coat than the kudu I had taken in South Africa.

We set about getting the truck back into the brush. I was amazed at the way they just plowed their way through. We grabbed some pictures and then loaded the bull into the bed of the truck. We headed back to camp feeling very satisfied with the hunt, until the giraffe attacked....

We were driving along, minding our own business and exchanging small talk, when all of a sudden Wayne jerked the steering wheel to the left and we lurched off the road. I glanced over at him and all I could see out the window was giraffe hide. He, she, or it had been feeding right beside the right side of the road. It didn't realize we were approaching until we were right on top of it. Instead of standing there to allow us to pass, or heading into the brush to the right, the beast decided that safety was on the left side of the road and didn't care if the source of its disruption was in the way. The huge animal bolted, or perhaps lumbered right at Wayne in the driver's seat, prompting his evasive maneuver. We crashed into the brush, the giraffe crashed into the brush beside us and the guys in the back held on for dear life. After it was over, we all had a good laugh, but I could just imagine that huge animal draped across the cab of the truck. How would you explain that one to your insurance company? Our complaints back home about bending a fender on a deer suddenly seemed trivial.

After fending off the giraffe, we made it back to camp unscathed and dropped the bull and the ram off at the skinning tent. Following lunch, Wayne departed to pick up his next client, who was after one of the big lions in the area. It was a great hunt, and I was sorry to see it come to an end. Wayne could not have been a better host. Although, while my hunt was over, I was staying in Zimbabwe for several more days until the rest of the party wrapped up their longer hunts.

Each day, if there was space in the truck, I'd tag along with Gary, Dave or Collins. I did some filming, took some pictures and generally just enjoyed being in Africa. One afternoon when I was camp bound, I loaded up the .375 and went for a walk down the riverbed, just to see what I could see. One of the PH's warned me about particularly nasty lion that he said would charge if I came upon him, hence the chamber full of three hundred grains of deterrent. There were also elephants and buffalo in the area, hence the three hundred grains of very solid deterrent in the chamber. It was actually very nice, as I found a kudu skull, some fish in one of the small ponds and other similar bits and pieces. One item that I tried desperately to ignore was several bicycle tracks in the sand. Why? Because I had not seen any bicycles in the area and those tracks were actually made by snakes, and it looked like some of those snakes were sporting those big balloon tires. As I related the story to the others later, there was some surprise that snakes could even ride bicycles. Maybe I was a little too excited relaying the facts …

I managed to make it back without meeting any of the creepy crawlers, but I must admit to looking at each step a little closer on the way back. That lion would have had to be chomping at my shoelaces for me to see him.

One morning I was riding along with Collins and his PH and we came across a fresh zebra kill. The lion had just begun to feed, when we came along spooking him from his meal. The PH looked at the tracks and figured that the zebra was taken by a good male. He began covering the zebra with brush to keep the vultures off with the intent to call Wayne and let him know that there was a ready made bait available for him. We were just climbing back into the truck, when the low rumbling grunt of a lion pierced the morning air a short way into the bush. He did not sound happy at all, and I was very pleased to get our intact skins out of there.

I rode around with the guys periodically and vicariously hunted sable, eland, kudu, buffalo, impala and warthog. I enjoyed the experience immensely. On the very last day, the four of us loaded into a truck and headed out to see if we could find Gary a sable. We didn't but we did get to see some hyenas, and we did get Dave an especially ugly warthog, which was a perfect way to end a memorable hunt.

Chapter 25

Leopard Charge
2006

I'll relate what I think is a suitable postscript to the previous couple of chapters. Wayne Williamson is as skilled a professional hunter as any who roam the planet. I would recommend him to anyone. But as good as he is, his chosen profession places him in constant danger. At the very beginning of my hunt, reports came in of a professional hunter the other PH's knew being killed by a buffalo. While I was in Zimbabwe, two professional hunters from our camp went into the bush after a wounded lion. They were charged from close quarters and managed to stop the big male before he could permanently rearrange any body parts. I lived with a small dose of this danger for a few days, generally as a second line of defense, but these guys live with the danger for years and they're always the first ones in. Sometimes, mostly in the case of wounded animals, they're the only ones going in to the bush. Sooner or later the odds are bound to catch up with them.

As I wrote the last chapter, Wayne Williamson was laying in a hospital bed with his head torn up and a crushed hand. He was helping another PH on a wounded leopard and got nailed. His story follows, first from his wife Muffy:

> Wayne spent three hours in theatre this afternoon, came out sore and shattered. His head looks like an axe murderer has mutilated it. He has a fractured bone in his left hand, they cannot set it as had to open it up to clean it. It is very swollen from that bad leopard's nasty bacteria!!!!! His shoulder left arm, and hand are really not functioning at all. Had a cat scan yesterday the skull is not fractured thank God.
>
> A French PH and his client wounded the leopard the night before. Wayne went in to help them. Wayne was crouching down when it came, it all happened very fast. The leopard hooked him on the right

side of the head and pulled Wayne's head into its mouth. Wayne some how got his hand and arm into its mouth to try and get it to stop eating his head. Wayne managed to throw the leopard off and the French PH shot it. This all happened in Mozambique. Wayne wrapped up his head on his own, organized the others to get the vehicle, then set his GPS and walked to the vehicle on his own—the thought of that makes me sick, I can't believe they let him walk on his own (he was probably being very bossy). They drove back to camp, got him into a boat, flew to Kariba for fuel and they came into Byo.

For some bizarre reason Wayne wrote out all his medical aid details that morning and gave them to the camp manager, he wrapped a towel around his left arm & duct taped it, he then put a leather glove on (he has never done that before)—that is the hand/arm that he shoved into the leopards mouth—the damage would have been far more severe without that protection. Wayne usually leaves his medical aid kit in the vehicle, he made his tracker carry it. The leopard literally scalped him, I cannot describe what his head looks like, no damage to his face or eyes.

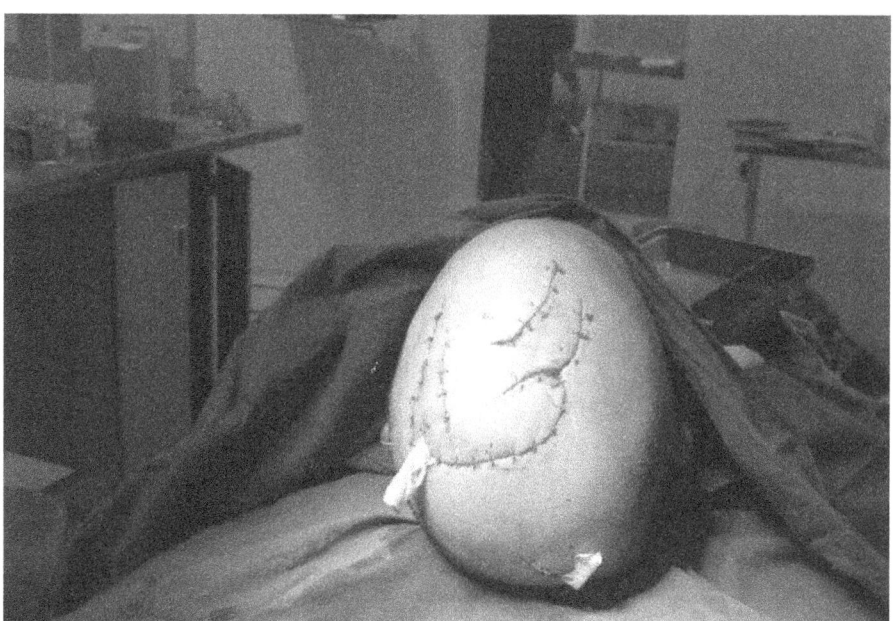

The damage a leopard can do in a split second, this is Wayne Williamson's head.

I hope this email makes sense, I am exhausted and not thinking very clearly. We hope to get Wayne to JHB tomorrow. He is being very brave, he honestly makes more fuss when he has the flu.
Then the story from Wayne's perspective:
The leopard was wounded on the Saturday evening, Wayne offered Yann his assistance on the follow up of the leopard in the morning. This is normal practice in a camp, PH's always help each other out. At six am the next morning they were on the trail. With very little blood to follow the tracking was slow, they had worked out that one of the legs had been shot, but they were not sure which one. Both Yann and Wayne were carrying shotguns, the trackers were carrying the heavy rifles. They tracked and caught up with the leopard at three pm Sunday afternoon. They were alerted to its presence by a troupe of baboons. They moved in hoping the baboons had distracted it, and they could shoot the leopard. The leopard charged, but due to long grass and thick bush they could not see it. The leopard could not get to them, so it then disappeared into a small gully. The tracker heard it and Wayne and Yann tried to get in ahead of it to cut it off. They heard it charging again. Wayne crouched down on his haunches to try to see under the leaves, it was very thick. The leopard broke cover but it was so quick neither Yann nor Wayne could get a bead on it, they both fired. By the time Wayne reloaded the cat was on him (it was later found the cat had been hit by a shotgun by some of the first shot). As Wayne was crouching down, it hooked its paw around his right ear and jaw, throwing him off balance. It then started biting and scratching Wayne's head. Wayne had wrapped padding around his left arm and was wearing a glove on his left hand. Wayne pried his left hand and arm into the leopard's mouth to stop it attacking his head. Once this was done he managed to roll the leopard off, within a fraction of a second of rolling it off, Yann managed to shoot it. Yann had wanted to shoot before, but wisely held back as he would have killed both Wayne and the leopard.
The leopard was then shot again to make sure it was dead. Wayne stood up, his scalp was flapped forward over his eyelids. Wayne placed his skin back into position and placed a trauma dressing over his head. Yann and Wayne then planned their next move. Yann would run with one tracker straight to the vehicle and bring it to the nearest point. Wayne had marked the road on his GPS

and Wayne would follow the GPS to the nearest point on the road. The remaining tracker and game scout would recover the leopard and other belongings, and then follow Wayne. The road was approximately one and a half kilometers. Wayne managed to get to the road before the trackers, and Yann later met Wayne there with the vehicle. On the way back to camp Yann drove and Wayne was on the radio to camp requesting they have bandages and antiseptic ready to tend to the wounds and try to stop the bleeding.

Simon Rodger (for who Wayne works) had landed in neighboring Zimbabwe (Kanyemba). Simon heard the radio conversation and started proceedings to keep airports open, and clear the route for Wayne to be flown back to Bulawayo for immediate medical assistance. Simon also managed to keep Kariba airport open for the aircraft to refuel. At this time Wayne was in camp, he poured anti septic over his head and onto a field dressing. This was strapped to his head. They continued to add bandages and towels to try to stem the bleeding. Wayne then got onto a boat accompanied by Sharon, the camp Manageress, who took care of Wayne and made sure the bleeding was under control. The boat trip was a fifty minute ride up the Zambezi River to Kanyemba in Zimbabwe. Simon was waiting with a vehicle to take Wayne to the airstrip. They took off at approximately five thirty in the evening, refueled in Kariba at last light using oil lamps on the runway to take off. They landed in Byo at eight that night, where Muffy was waiting with the Mars ambulance. Wayne was in casualty by eight thirty that night. Wayne has had two sets of surgery on his head and left hand at the Mater Dei Hospital, and whilst in a lot of pain is making a good recovery.

Imagine my surprise when just a few short weeks after being notified of Wayne's brush with the angry kitty, I received an email from Wayne stating that he was back in the bush guiding clients. That, my friends, is one tough hombre.

Chapter 26
Golden Gate Elk in the High Country
2005 & 2006

As I looked through my spotting scope at the feeding bull he turned sideways and lifted his head showing me all I needed to see. He was a basic six point with nice long tines and good width to his frame. I put the range finder on him and he was right at four hundred yards. From an absolutely solid rest, that's not a difficult shot for me and I could feel my heart pounding in my chest. The bull was well above us, and allowing for the angle, I quickly figured that I should hold for three hundred yards. Once again the fall found me in the Colorado Rockies.

I drove in behind Holly Christensen in my rental roller-skate, struggling to keep up with what I guessed to be the three and a half horsepower inboard/outboard under the hood. The first thing that struck me was snow. There was a lot of snow on the ground, which is good for some things, but bad for elk hunting in the area I was being led to. It's also bad for roller skates. When the snow hits the high country, the elk head for better pastures. That meant that my hunt could be nothing but a week of making snowmen.

Randy Christensen had talked me into an elk hunt in the high country with promises of big bulls behind every tree. At least that's what I think he said, I was too entranced with the picture of the three hundred and sixty point bull he had taken to really pay any attention to what he was saying. Shortly after arriving, I met my guide who was Randy's son in law, Steve McCollum. He was young, thin, long legged, lived up around Mount Everest elevation, and didn't need to breath on the weekends. You know the type, just a despicable human being; I didn't like him right away. Randy was leasing a large chunk of land about twenty miles west of Denver. The land was mainly timber, with a few open parks scattered around randomly.

We went to the range, and made sure the 300 Win Mag was still on after the flight. After that we went up into the mountains for a little scouting foray. We parked the truck and dropped over a hill above a small park. Immediately, we could hear elk below us. After a brief encounter with a small mulie, we dropped down to the elk. We located a herd of cows, a rag horn and a big bull with six points on one side and a broken main beam about half way up on the other side. It was a good walk, and filled me with expectations for the morning. As we talked that afternoon, I told Steve that with the potential of the area, I was looking for a good mature six point, and if I went home empty handed, that's just the way it goes.

The first day out, Steve stole Randy's new jeep (I was beginning to like him more and more) and drove as far up into the mountains as we could and then started trudging through the snow. We were headed down a hill, when we spotted an elk on an adjacent ridge. Some glassing revealed two elk. One was a rag horn and the other about a two hundred and seventy point six by six. I really didn't think about it very long, he needed another year or two under his belt, so we kept on walking. We walked down to an open hillside, glassed it over really well and then Steve turned and gave me that look that told me we now had to go back up the hill. I noticed that he had forgotten the oxygen bottles, and made a mental note to mention that to him if I made it back to the jeep.

I don't remember much about the climb back, but then without any oxygen reaching my brain that's to be expected. We returned to the cabin for the middle of the day, which is a pattern we repeated almost every day, since the elk were not active at that time. To make matters worse, there was a full moon and clear skies, so the elk were feeding all night long and returning to the heavy cover to bed fairly early in the morning.

That afternoon we found another hill to climb up, then down the other side, and then back up again. We located some cows and a rag horn about a mile off, but that was it. It was fairly uneventful and we returned to camp that evening to plan for the next day. We decided to glass from below the next morning.

We were up early and out the door well before daylight, to try and catch the elk before they retreated for the day. The first few hillsides we glassed produced nothing, and the morning was well along when we saw a cow on the hillside. That cow became many, and soon a bull emerged from the timber into the opening. At first glance, even from six hundred yards, there seemed to be a lot of bone on his head, shining in the sunlight. Some of the bone disappeared when we put the glasses on him however. One beam was almost completely broken off. The other beam held six points, and he was a very nice mature bull, but I wasn't really interested in a bull that just went in circles. We returned to camp, and Randy mentioned something about the wonderful things taxidermists can do with broken antlers. At least that's what I think he said, I was looking at the picture of him with that three sixty bull, so I wasn't really listening.

That afternoon we went to one of Steve's favorite places, a big open park in the middle of the timber. There are a series of rock outcroppings where you can set up and glass, with the park well below. The furthest shot would be about four hundred and fifty yards and the rocks provided a perfect bench rest. Upon arrival, Steve immediately located a five by five bull below us. After the spots stopped dancing in front of my eyes, I could see him also. A few cows and calves fed along the edge as well, and then wandered into the timber.

Steve had gone down the ridgeline to glass the park from a little different angle when elk started pouring out of the far timberline at a run. The adrenaline kicked in as antlers flashed in the glasses. In total about twenty elk trotted out, with three young bulls in the bunch. About then, Steve came running up the hill as excited about what was happening as I was. We sat and glassed, waiting for big boy to show up, but he never made an appearance. Eventually, the elk fed out of the park and onto a trail that came within about eighty yards of us in the thick timber. I kept the rifle trained on a single opening, just in case they had picked up some company, to no avail.

We returned to camp after an eventful day with a full moon rising and warmer temperatures arriving. Shortly before my arrival, a large snowstorm had come through dumping a good amount of snow on the ground. It had Randy so nervous that the elk had left the area that he sent Steve out to see if there were any tracks in the snow. There were, so apparently the elk had taken a vote and decided to stay in the area. But now, the snow was melting as temperatures increased. Warm temperatures coupled with a full moon promised a difficult conclusion to our hunt.

The third morning of the hunt found us right back at the same spot we had left the previous evening. We arrived just in time to see the broken horned bull we saw the day before the hunt walk out of the park bugling his head off. Randy had mentioned how good the taxidermists were again at last night's dinner, but I chose to ignore him. We got a call that Randy's other client had wounded a monster bull, and Steve went to see if he could offer some assistance. Being a die hard whitetail hunter, I told Steve to go ahead, and I'd spend the day on the ridgeline to see if there was any mid day movement at all. It was incredibly windy, and it hammered me all day, but I stuck it out and saw one small bull for my trouble. Steve and a friend ended up tracking the wounded bull for about five miles, and never caught sight of him. It was a somber group that made it back to camp that night. I was just happy they remembered me, it would have been a long walk back to camp.

The fourth morning was uneventful, with us not seeing a single elk. The afternoon got interesting though. Randy found a good bull with a group of spikes. As I said at the beginning of the chapter, after looking at him through the scope, I knew I had found the bull that I came for. Then Randy rained on my parade. He told me that he didn't think I should shoot the bull because he was on an extremely steep rocky hillside, and if I dropped him there, he'd be nothing but elk parts by the time he hit the bottom. Have I mentioned that I hate gravity?

The evening leaked away and we left in the gathering gloom, hoping to come back in the morning to find the bull again. On a good note, some clouds moved in, covering that bleeping moon. The next morning some snow rolled in and we were out early glassing all the hillsides in the area. We actually saw quite a few elk, and a few five point bulls, but big boy had disappeared. We spent most of the day looking for him, but never saw another hair. I could have shot one of the five points, but they were young and needed a few more years to be mature. I ended my hunt without firing a shot, yet I enjoyed the adventure thoroughly.

That night, Randy was going on about good taxidermists, hunting next year and something about scratches on his jeep. At least I think that's what he was talking about, I wasn't really listening, he had that picture out again....

The year passed quickly, and once again Randy was responsible for a summer of pain. There was biking, walking up and down hills with weights on my back, and not eating cake. It was brutal. Hopefully it would all be worth it. Since I was doubling my pleasure by guiding for Randy for mule deer after my elk hunt, I had driven my truck across the country, stopping periodically to rob a bank to pay for gas. After making the mandatory stop at Cabelas, I got into Denver mid morning a couple of days before the beginning of the hunt. I wasn't due in to camp till the afternoon so I decided to stretch my legs after a few days in the truck. It was a nice sunny crisp day so I took a hike about a thousand feet up a mountain and reacquainted myself with the lack of oxygen.

When I arrived at the cabin, Randy and Holly were already there. We got caught up with each other, I unloaded the truck and got settled in. I then went out in search of a cell phone signal, which was kind of like finding a bass in a pike convention. Upon my return I met cook Tim Winter. Over the next day and a half we went out and did some scouting. We found a three hundred sixty class bull on the side of a mountain just off the property and a three hundred class bull right on the border. Somewhere along the way, Derek Barner arrived in camp as the other hunter for the week.

The first morning out was crisp and clear. Randy walked me up a mountain, starting directly from camp. As a change of pace, Randy had set up several tree stands in the area, and I got to try one first hand. I sat in the stand till mid morning having seen nothing, then headed back to camp. In the afternoon I walked back up to the same stand in the rain and again had the same results. Derek didn't fair much better in a stand further down the hill. Randy, Tim and Steve however did see a herd of elk including two big bulls cross the road headed towards our leased land shortly after sunset.

The next morning was again crisp and clear as I made my way up to the tree stand. Shortly after sunrise I caught some movement in the brush down the hill ahead of me. Then, I saw a definite outline of a rack. My heart rate increased dramatically as the bull stepped into the clear just over a hundred yards off. I picked up my glasses and took a look at the animal. There's no doubt that he was a good bull with a nice wide spread and five points on each main beam. I took a good hard look at him as he closed the distance to eighty yards, but he simply was not the bull I had come to Colorado to take. He turned down the hill toward Derek and I waited for the inevitable. The shot never came, the bull had somehow gotten by him without being detected. The afternoon brought no sightings.

The next morning was a carbon copy of the previous and I again returned to the same tree stand. About mid morning I caught movement in the brush. Elk were filtering through moving diagonally toward me. Cows and calves made their way into the open area below me as I scanned the bush for the bull that was sure to follow. The small herd of a dozen animals single filed their way in front of me, then suddenly spooked and ran directly under my tree up the hill. When I got back to camp, one of the other guys who was watching from below about a mile away said that there was a big six point with the group, but he had broken off and turned up the hill a couple hundred yards from me. It seemed that my trend in elk hunting luck was following a familiar pattern. That afternoon I tried a different stand to no avail, although Derek at least got a shot at a bull higher on the mountain with indeterminate results. The weather was beginning to change with some snow in the air and a stiff wind.

The fourth day of the hunt was the calm before the storm, as over a foot of snow was predicted for the day. Randy and I drove high up the mountain to listen for any bugling bulls down below. Of course, we could hear a bull bugling down by the tree stand where I had spent my first couple of days. We drove back down, then worked our way fairly close and called, but he was not leaving his cows and there was no easy approach for his location in the thick timber. We decided to leave him alone and not spook him, hoping for a better opportunity later on. We left him, jumped into the truck and headed up again. As we turned around one of the switchbacks my eyes got wide as we saw two bulls within shooting distance of the tree stand I was in the previous evening. One of the bulls looked very good, so Randy dumped me out on the side of the road and I stalked the area. I got there just in time to see the flash of a bull through the trees three hundred yards away. I flopped down on my belly and searched ahead with my scope. I never saw another glimpse. Randy said that the bull he saw was a big one, and probably a shooter.

We ended up near the top of the mountain with a fairly large park directly below us. Randy made a few cow calls and he was immediately answered by a bull three hundred yards directly below us. I got set up on the bipod as Randy continued to call. The bull answered in a low guttural growl and we could hear him working his way toward us. He came right to the edge of the timber, but would not step into the open. He eventually started back down the hill to his cows.

Following that bit of excitement, I headed back to the tree stand for the remainder of the morning. I got three bugles from the heavy timber as I cow called, but the bull eventually moved away. The snow began at about eight as predicted and by the time I headed for camp at eleven it was really coming down. A few hours later found Tim and Darren headed up the hill in the jeep. The ground was still warm and the snow turned to ice as soon as they drove over it. They were back in camp in less than an hour, saying that it was simply too dangerous. Darren headed for one of the tree stands on foot while Randy and I decided to work the timber directly above camp. By the time we started up the hill, there was about a foot of snow on the ground and it was coming down hard enough to make me homesick for the lake effect snow back in New York.

We worked the timber slowly, stopping to call occasionally. Randy's first call woke up a red squirrel, and his second got a response from a train. The third time was the charm as a bull answered from below us. Once again, the bull hung up, not wanting to leave his cows. We closed the distance as close as we dared, but the bull was in the thick stuff and there was no way to get to him. We new they'd head for the field as the sun set, so we left him alone and continued to work the hill. We eventually made it to the field and found Darren in the upper tree stand, so I backed off and headed for the bottom stand as Randy stayed to call. As the snowy dusk descended, the herd came out below me, and I was again faced with a nice 5x5 bull within shooting range. Even with the hunt headed for an end, I let him walk. Randy and Darren popped over the hill and the herd headed back into the timber. They had seen nothing up above, and Darren said he would have shot that bull in a heartbeat.

Once again I was faced with the dawn of a final day of elk hunting. The morning was cold, but at least the snow had stopped. Several additional inches had fallen overnight leaving about a foot and a half of snow on the ground. Randy and I again went high, as Darren stayed low. The elk had completely abandoned the upper portions of the ranch, and I wondered if they had left the property all together. This question was answered as a bugle sounded from the area around my tree stand.

Randy dropped me off above the stand and I slowly made my way down the hill glassing every little opening as I went. After about twenty minutes of playing cat and mouse I suddenly spotted movement through the brush about a hundred yards away. Through my glasses I could make out antlers and my heart rate increased dramatically. I worked my way closer until I could make out the animal and found that he was just a rag horn. I continued down the hill at a crawl and ended up walking right into the middle of a herd. For over an hour I moved when I could, trying to get to the bull bugling just over the ridgeline. The cold dry weather helped mask my scent until a calf got to within twenty yards of me directly down wind. She spooked, ran about twenty yards then turned around to see what the problem was. Not seeing me, she settled back down and started feeding again. I never could get to the bull, there were simply too many cows and calves in the way. Eventually, the herd wandered off the lease and I retreated to the tree stand.

I hadn't been there long when there were several shots from below. Darren had a big group of elk all around him and had taken a rag horn. I later learned that at the shot, the spooked elk started running across the hill. As they ran they picked up more and more elk until a huge herd was in motion. Unfortunately for me, they ended up running right off the lease. Back at the cabin, we decided to do some long range glassing in the afternoon and make a move on a bull if we saw one. We went out and glassed, but it was pretty obvious that the elk had cleared out. Another elk season was at an end. Some would say that my hunt had been unsuccessful, but I really enjoyed myself and it only made me more determined to take a big bull. I'll be back. After all the third time has got to be the charm, right?

Chapter 27

Canadian Drops and Kickers
2005

Reprinted from the Journal of Safari Big Game Hunting Magazine

The small buck looked back over his shoulder and I followed his gaze. Through my binoculars I caught movement and glimpsed a dark rack about two hundred and fifty yards through the trees. As the buck slowly made his way toward me I could see a big body and a decent frame to his rack. He hit a small clearing and I immediately saw that he sported a drop tine on his right side. That did it, I hit the adrenaline button, dropped the glasses and grabbed the rifle.

    I was hunting the famed Mosquito Indian Reservation in West central Saskatchewan with Charles Stone Outfitting. Two years prior to this hunt had found me in a similar blind on the reservation watching a huge bodied buck break over a ridge about three hundred yards away. In twenty never mind years of hunting, he was by far the biggest bodied deer I'd ever seen. He sported four points on each side, and his antler mass matched his body, even up through the tines. I never hesitated, I steadied the crosshairs on his shoulder at two hundred and seventy yards and squeezed the trigger. After a somewhat adventurous tracking job I approached the downed buck, and wondered if I was going to be in trouble for not having a moose tag. I've taken a few bucks that dressed out just over two hundred pounds, but this thing was beyond my estimating ability. Later, in the skinning shed, one of the guides remarked about the large body. I had not brought my scale, so I asked him how much he figured it would dress out. He casually said, "Oh, he will be between two hundred eighty and three hundred pounds." Stunned, I thought to myself that any animal that size should be wearing a saddle. Later, when I mounted the buck, I bought the biggest manikin I could find, and still could have bulked up the shoulders some more. Following that experience, I vowed to return.

The monster Canadian eight point next to a more "normal" sized buck. No, this isn't "photoshopped".

So I was back, in early November to find a brand new log home, and very comfortable accommodations. Charles Stone runs a fine operation for whitetails, and he has the most impressive privately owned collection of antlers I've ever seen. I quickly got settled in, and prepared for the next day's hunt.

The first day found me about fifteen feet up in a tower blind on a cut line overlooking a vast area of brush. In the past, I'd found Saskatchewan that time of year to be cold enough to freeze the dimples off a golf ball. But it was a balmy 20F, with a projected high near freezing. That's practically beach weather up there. I started seeing deer right away, but mostly at a great distance. About mid morning a half rack five point pushed some does past the stand. A spike ran around like a puppy, chasing anything that moved for a few hours. Early in the afternoon I saw some movement in the thick stuff in front of the stand. A nice one hundred thirty class 4x5 buck walked by at about sixty yards, with his nose to the ground and tail at half mast. He wasn't quite what I was after, so I decided to see if I could bring him closer for some pictures. I grunted at him and got his attention after the third try. He came to me like I owed him money, stopping occasionally to abuse an innocent bush and ending up directly below me. He paused at the bottom of the tower presumably trying to figure out how to climb the ladder. Eventually, he got bored and wandered off. I continued to see does for the rest of the day, ending up with a count of something like seventy of them.

The next day, I ended up back at the same stand I had shot the massive eight point from. As the dreary day started to lighten, a group of coyotes opened up a few hundred yards in front of me. Shortly after that, a doe ran across in front of me with a coyote right behind. About ten minutes later I saw movement in front of me, and it was another coyote. I started to make squeaking sounds and ended up with three coyotes coming in for a free meal. Two of them had gone by me, when the third caught sight of a deer and took off after it, joined by the other two. All I saw of the deer was a flag. That was not a good start to the day, and then the fog rolled in, often limiting my vision to only fifty yards or so. It was a long day in the stand staring at the haze and I saw no deer until right before sunset, when the fog lifted. I ended up seeing a dozen does, two small bucks and two more coyotes. Back at the house we discussed the coyote activity. There was some concern since the coyotes don't normally pack up and pursue deer until later in the winter.

On the third day I was in a new blind well before daylight started to creep in from the east. As it began to get light, I could just make out movement in the gloom about a hundred fifty yards out. A narrow old 4x4 and a nice wide 5x6 sparred with each other, neither one getting too serious about it. The 5x6 had my attention and probably would have been in the mid one forty's, but I decided to pass on him and let him get another year under his belt. The morning passed fairly uneventfully except for a few does. Somewhere around lunch time, I was busy filling a bottle the best way I knew how and saw movement about a hundred yards away.... antlers! I uttered the standard phrases one might expect at a moment like that, and got my ... uh ... self together as quickly as possible. The buck stepped into an opening and revealed himself to be a young 4x4. I was continuing to swear at him for good measure when he stopped and looked behind him. That's when the drop tine buck made his entrance. I've never had a chance at a drop tined buck, so as soon as I found an opening, I squeezed the trigger, and my Browning Stainless Stalker jumped in my hands. The buck ran about forty yards and crashed to the ground. I took a walk over to find a very unique 5x6 with a drop on one side and a kicker on the other. Following standard procedure I walked to a designated spot and tied some flagging to a tree, indicating to the guide that at the next check I wanted him to walk in to the stand. After about a half hour, guide Brad Strandquist accompanied by tagged out hunter Ralph Dischler arrived at the blind. I said to Brad through chattering teeth, "I'm freezing, I've got to get out of here." There was a shocked look on his face, since he knew I was equipped for a polar expedition, but he recovered quickly and said, "Okay, let's go." I started to gather up my gear, and added, "But we should probably get my deer first." He somehow restrained himself from hitting me, and we had a good laugh over it. I spent the next few days exploring the reservation, and then headed to my first hunt in Alberta.

Author with a great Canadian drop tine buck.

I arrived at the main lodge of Alberta Trophy Hunts just south of Edmonton, and met owners Fran and Stan Reiser. They've got several two person cabins, a bathhouse and a main lodge. They outfit for waterfowl, moose, whitetails, mule deer and fish. There were eight people in camp on my hunt with a mixture of whitetail and moose hunters.

Stan had seen a B&C 5x5 enter a patch of woods the previous evening where he had a box blind, so the morning found me making the three quarter mile trek into the bush. It was very windy and warm with the temperature hovering just below freezing. It was a slow day, with only one little 3x4 making an appearance about mid day. Back at the lodge, we discussed our options, and while I was willing to put in another day at the same stand for a buck like that, Stan decided to move me to tree stand where they had seen another monster. Guide Clint Reiser showed me a picture of the buck and he was one of those deer that doesn't require any evaluation or decision making, just shooting.

So the next morning I walked about four hundred yards down a cut line, climbed into the stand and got settled in. Mid morning a one twenty class 4x5 walked by about twenty-five yards out, then a spike slid by about a hundred yards in the opposite direction. About an hour later I caught trotting legs about a hundred yards through the trees. Three does came through, obviously being pushed. I got the gun up and ready and pretty soon there was more movement. Unfortunately it was just a small six point. Not too long after that I heard crashing brush in the thick stuff behind the stand. I stood and got myself turned around. After several minutes three does burst from the cover and scattered around the stand. After standing and looking back for a few minutes they began to wander off. The does were long gone and I was about ready to sit back down when I heard an animal trotting toward me. A buck plowed through the heavy cover fifty yards away with his nose to the ground. I could tell immediately that he had good mass, ten long points and long main beams. I decided to go ahead and take him, but in the thick cover I needed to get him to slow down or stop. He evidently had serious plans, and didn't even break stride as I grunted at him. In a few seconds the brush swallowed him. Just as I thought he was gone for good, he broke back out of the cover and came right back in my direction. He ended up close enough to consider roping him as an option, but I decided on the .300 Win Mag. I took the shot as he ran by the tree at about five yards.

He made a quick fifty yard sprint and I heard him pile up. I dumped half my stuff over the side of the blind and made a sprint of my own over to where the buck was. He was just what I thought he was, a good mature 5x6 with a kicker off the left base, a good buck in anybody's book.

After checking to make sure he was down, I called Clint. Never missing an opportunity to maintain my normal behavioral pattern of being somewhat of a smart … um … alleck, I told him in a loud voice that I was just calling to see if anyone else was seeing anything. I could hear the confusion and unanswered questions in his voice when he told me very professionally that he really hadn't heard anything and wouldn't be aware of what the other hunters were seeing. I then informed him that I was also calling because I needed some help getting a deer out of the woods. It was at that point that I decided that using a cell phone was definitely better than having your guide within striking distance.

Author with an Alberta 5x6 taken at spear throwing distance.

Chapter 28
A Guide's Life
2006

I slammed on the brakes as I rounded the corner and saw the bulls on the ridgeline several hundred yards ahead of us. "There they are," I hissed between my teeth. Nick bailed out the passenger side of the truck. I grabbed my pack and we were soon belly crawling along our own ridgeline toward the last place we had seen the bulls. As we broke into the open, we could see two bulls below us, the third was nowhere to be seen. I pushed my pack in front of Nick and manned my binoculars. The first bull was a massive 5x4 that one of the other guides had seen prior to the season. One side of his rack had the classic typical five points, with very good mass. The other side started out the same way at the base, but then topped out with a huge sword. The other bull was a rag horn. Nick said he was going to shoot the first bull as soon as he turned.

Once again I found myself on the front range of the Rockies just west of Golden Colorado with Golden Gate Outfitters. There was a difference this time however. Following an elk hunt in the high country as a client with Randy Christensen, I had made the conversion to one of his guides on the scenic ten thousand acre ranch. It was the same ranch I had hunted since 1997, and had taken that thirty-one inch monster mulie a few years back. After taking that buck, I figured that there was nothing to do then, except to hang up the gun and pick up the spotting scope to help other hunters take a big old buck.

The day before the season found us with four hunters instead of the anticipated six. Bad news for two, good news for four. We ended up with Nick Hill, Karl Savoie, Kent Fagan and Bruce Matthews. Fellow guide Steve McCollum and I took the guys off the ranch to a shooting bench to make sure the rifles were still on after the plane ride. On the way back, we entered the center of the ranch right at sunset. There were deer everywhere, including a few good bucks. In fact I had never seen that concentration of deer anywhere on the ranch. We had probably seen eighty deer and a few elk during the fifteen minute ride back to the ranch house.

It takes some snow in the high country to drive the elk down onto the ranch. In recent years the snow just hasn't been there, but a snow storm a few weeks prior had done its job and there were elk on the ranch, including at least one bull that Steve had seen that was pushing three hundred and fifty points. Knowing that there were elk on the ranch, and also knowing how quickly they can disappear, Randy talked to the hunters to see if any of them wanted to try for elk in the morning. Three of them did, so we decided to concentrate on spotting for elk in the morning.

Nick climbed into my truck before sunrise the next morning and three vehicles paraded down the road that bisects the ranch. We stopped at a good vantage point and began glassing as the gray dawn began to brighten the surrounding hills. No elk.... not a single solitary animal showed itself where they had been seen previously. So much for our plans, it was time to improvise. Randy said that he'd take Karl, and Steve would take Bruce to different parts of the ranch. Nick and I would cover the general area we were already in. I had finished glassing the hills about a half mile away and told Nick that I was going to get the spotting scope and cover the bare hills about a mile away. Before I could even open the door to the truck, Nick said, "There they are." Three bulls were on the bare hillside, working their way toward the bottom. After a quick look through the spotting scope we jumped into the truck and headed for the bulls.

That's when we were delayed by an unexpected turn of events. A herd of mule deer appeared a quarter mile ahead of us. There were a few dozen does and several bucks. One of them was a wide buck that we had seen the previous evening. A frantic discussion followed on what we should do. The question at hand was that if we went after the elk, would the deer still be there and visa versa. With that "bird in the hand" thing in mind, we decided to try for the deer first. We quickly closed the distance on the herd, holding our breaths as some of the younger bucks pushed the does around making them skittish. We eventually worked below the herd and my range finder said just under two hundred yards. Three of the bucks were walking together and I warned Nick to be careful about which buck he was aiming at. Once we agreed on the right buck, Nick settled in and took the shot. The buck humped up at the shot, walked a few steps and went down.

The next few minutes were a blur as we sprinted up the slope to make sure the buck was down. My breathe came in gasps in the thin air as we quickly admired the buck, then headed back down the hill to see if we could get back on those elk. Pictures could wait.

We found the elk as described earlier. I frantically looked for the third bull and tried to talk Nick into waiting to see if we could find him. Nick wanted no part of that talk, and frankly I didn't blame him, this was a very unique, large bodied, mature bull. Knowing that bullets were about to be launched regardless of the location of the third bull, I grabbed my range finder and told Nick that the bull was about three hundred and fifty yards. He settled in on the pack and squeezed the trigger. The solid wallop resounded back at us as the bull bucked and started running directly toward us. Nick took another shot, and a few follow up shots later we were standing next to the bull.

The sun was barely up and we had taken two very respectable animals. Some parts of the ranch require animals to be packed out, but we were able to drive a mule (gas powered, not hay powered) to both animals. We ended up with both animals back to camp and skinned in time for lunch.

That afternoon and the next morning we spotted for the other hunters, but didn't locate any shooter bucks. During the middle of the day, we took care of the meat then spotted again in the evening. Following a great meal prepared by camp cook Tim Winter, Randy decided that I had had enough time off and it was time to get back to work, so he asked me to take Karl to the east part of the ranch the next morning.

Karl and I headed to the North East part of the ranch in the morning. We spotted several deer fairly quickly including a nice buck a half mile away down in Hell's Canyon. Yes, it is as bad as it sounds, and it would have a stronger name except that they couldn't think of one at the time. Karl spotted another good buck in the canyon, but he was in a position that made it difficult to get a good look at him. We side hilled into the mouth of the canyon a few hundred yards to get a better look. As I looked through the spotting scope I could tell that he was a decent 4x4, but probably not a shooter. Then I noticed a point that came off the base of one antler and extended several inches beside the buck's nose.

Karl took a look through the scope and debated whether or not he wanted the buck. We talked about the effort it would take to get to the buck and what he really looked like. At one point I thought we were in for a couple hour hike into the canyon and started to strip out of my warm gear, but Karl finally decided to leave the buck and look for something else. We saw several more good bucks but no shooters until we went to the southeast portion of the ranch. As I glassed the brush at the bottom of Hell's Canyon, I could see several deer including a few bucks. Then, I spotted the outline of a rack in the brush and immediately told Karl that we needed to get the spotting scope on that buck.

The buck was very nice with decent fronts, good backs with one double split, good mass and a spread in the low twenties. Karl and I debated on that buck for a good twenty minutes. With a few more days to hunt Karl decided to pass and look for something better, and maybe on flatter terrain. For some reason, bucks always look just a little bit smaller when they're at the bottom of Hell's Canyon.

That afternoon we headed to the western part of the ranch to glass a drainage that would have been named Hell's Canyon, if that name hadn't already been taken. We didn't see anything in the drainage, but walking back to the truck, Karl spotted a deer in the brush a quarter mile away. I got the spotting scope on the buck for a split second as he chased a doe around. My impression was of a buck with a spread in the high twenties with good height. I turned to Karl and said, "This buck definitely has my attention."

In the standard "hunker" position, we headed for the brushy draw where we had last seen the buck. We stopped periodically to glass, with a false alarm caused by a smaller buck in the drainage. As we closed to about three hundred yards we could see the smaller buck and another deer feeding in the brush. After a few moments the second deer cleared the brush and I could see that he was indeed very good. He was wide, pushing thirty inches, and he was very tall. He had everything you'd ever want in a mule deer, except that his fronts were just crab claws. Reluctantly we left him and headed back to the truck.

We then headed for a section that we called the horseshoe, because, well, it's shaped like a horseshoe. There was a group of does and a big bodied buck on the hillside. The buck's body was huge, he had deep tall back tines, and a lot of mass. I figured he was only twenty to twenty one inches with a decent front on one side and a crab claw on the other. He was definitely a good buck, but with another few days to hunt, we decided to pass.

The next morning dawned warm with sustained winds of forty to fifty miles an hour with gusts to seventy-five miles an hour. Karl said that back home in New Orleans when the wind gets that high they'd put a name on it. We headed west and saw a few good bucks, but with the warm temperatures and wind they were already bedded at first light. It was not a good sign. We headed back to the horseshoe, and the same big bodied buck was still there. All of a sudden another big buck broke over the hill and started heading for the big boy's does. He wasn't quite a shooter, but a nice buck none the less. With the rut starting to crank up, I remarked to Karl that that would be just how quickly a big buck could present himself for a shot. It's interesting to note that on the trip back, he was nowhere to be seen.

We then headed down into a deep drainage with very steep slopes and an access road just slightly bigger than the truck. We saw one small buck, duplicating what the other guys were seeing. The area was normally a big buck hot spot, and Randy felt like a lion had taken up residence in the area. At one point we saw a flock of magpies on one of the hillsides, confirming Randy's sentiment. The trip back up was interesting with Karl falling noticeably silent, and immobile. Apparently, being on the side of the truck where the ground falls away for hundreds of feet had some kind of physiological effect. He regained consciousness upon reaching the summit and remarked that if we saw a Boone and Crocket buck down there, the buck could die of old age, because we were not going back down. He said some more that I didn't quite follow, but I did pick out words like, "crazy", "idiotic" and "stupid".

We looked in a few other places and saw some deer, but they were mostly bedded out of the wind. After a quick stop back at the lodge, Karl decided that he wanted to try for that nice 5x4 down in Hell's Canyon. On the way there we saw a heavy horned buck, but he had high forks so we kept on going. Of course, now that we were looking for the 5x4 he was nowhere to be found, so we decided to see if we could locate that wide crab claw buck. We ended up with the same luck. With two strikes against us we then went to see if we could locate the heavy horned buck that was in the horseshoe. As the sun began to drop behind the mountains, we found him. He was right where we had left him before, and Karl decided to go ahead and take him.

I ranged the buck at around two hundred yards and Karl prepared for the shot. As he squeezed the trigger the report of the rifle was followed by the solid thump of the bullet reaching its intended target. The buck kicked and started around the hill. I was pretty sure of a good hit, but told Karl to hit him again if he wanted to. He did, and one more shot put the buck down for good.

Hunter Karl Savoie with his brute of a mule deer.

As I walked up to the buck he kept getting bigger and bigger. When I finally reached him, I knew Karl had something special on his hands. The buck was by far the biggest bodied buck I had ever seen, he was absolutely huge. He was so big that his shadow weighed ten pounds. The "good mass" that I thought he had, became "great mass" and while he didn't suddenly become a thirty inch buck, he was also a few inches wider than I thought. I later measured his ear span, and it was a full twenty-four inches, which is very big for a mulie in that area and explained my underestimating the spread.

After some backslapping and congratulations, I quickly grabbed my camera and took a number of pictures in the fading light. We then had the monumental task of loading him into my truck, which we managed with colorful words and slipped discs in our backs.

The next morning we went out and glassed to the east to see if we could find Kent a good buck. We actually did spot two nice bucks but never could catch up to guide Mike Smith and Kent to convey the information. I didn't really matter, however since they ended up taking a very nice 4x4 late in the morning. It was a fitting end to a great week in Colorado.

This might be a suitable spot to mention Glenn's guide to guided hunts. I've spent most of my life in the woods and have a definite way I like to hunt, and certain opinions about what works and what doesn't. Frankly, I prefer to hunt alone as I found that I'm generally slower when still hunting, more patient when stand hunting and a more thorough glasser. Even with a client along I tend to rush my glassing more than I would when alone. With all of that said however, if you go on a guided hunt with an open mind and a small dose of tolerance, it can make for a very enjoyable hunt. You also never know if you might learn something new along the way.

Why go on a guided hunt at all? Because the guys that know what they're doing manage the property they're hunting for mature animals. They also restrict access to the property or hunt an area that's difficult for others to access so you don't have an orange vest behind every tree. It's hard to find much of that on public land, and it's really difficult for an out of stater to properly research and scout land that's hundreds of miles away. You also generally find people with the same interests as you, and life long friendships can be formed. Occasionally you might run into some big egos attached to big money, but I've found this to be the exception rather than the rule. Most guys (and gals) are there because they love to hunt, just like you.

Generally speaking, like most things in life, you get what you pay for. I've heard of bargain basement hunts in Canada that sounded too good to be true. When I started asking questions, like how many acres do you hunt and how many hunters do you put through them, the math told the story of definite over hunting. Then I asked how many repeat hunters they had. There was a certain lag in their response, and they couldn't come up with any names for me to contact. That was a huge red flag, and pretty much ended the conversation. Did they shoot some good bucks and have pretty pictures on their web sites? Absolutely, at the rate of about one big buck every three years.

How do you avoid a bad outfitter? I've found that going through a reputable agent helps ensure that you're getting a quality hunt. You don't pay any more for their services, and their reputations are dependent on providing their clients with great adventures. Give the outfitter a call, and ask questions like those above and get a list of successful and unsuccessful hunters to contact. They're generally more than willing to share the good, bad and the ugly that happened on their hunts.

So, the next challenge is how the heck does the average person pay thousands of dollars to go on a guided hunt? For me it was simple, I made going on these hunts a big priority in my life and set aside money every paycheck without fail. You'd be surprised how quickly you can save money with that kind of plan. A friend of mine quit smoking several years ago, and we figured that if he put the same amount of money away as he was spending on cigarettes, he could go up to Canada with me every couple of years. Most smokers make cigarettes a priority, and figure out a way to pay for cigarettes. I do the same thing with hunting trips.

I find that it's a more enjoyable trip, if you just go with the flow much of the time. Expect delays at borders, flight delays and the occasionally vehicle breakdown. Remember, outfitters are people too, and things don't always go as planned.

Chapter 29
Nebraska Ducks and Bucks
2006

I sat and watched as the doe and fawn fed across the clearing a couple hundred yards away. They never looked back or gave any other indication that they were being harassed by a buck. I started to turn in another direction when some movement caught my eye. A buck had burst out of the cover fifty yards beyond the does and was making a bee line in their direction, trotting along with his head down low. I quickly brought my binoculars into action. The first thing that caught my eye was that his rack was well outside his ears, with a spread of over twenty inches. Almost at the same instant I saw his brow tines that were taller than anything I had ever seen before. Then I glanced at the antler bases and they looked like they were trying to grow together like the boss on a cape buffalo. All of this took perhaps two seconds and all it really meant to me was that I could forget about any further analysis because he was a "shooter" for sure.

Following my stint guiding for mule deer and elk in Colorado I had arrived a few days earlier after driving across the plains toward South Western Nebraska. The wind howled as I drove along, triggering a mass migration of tumbleweed. It almost became a game, trying to miss them as they shot across the road. I'm afraid I left tumbleweed parts all over the road for about a hundred miles. I was hunting with Western Nebraska Waterfowl owned and operated by Jerry and Karen Eggers. The next question of course might be why on earth I was hunting whitetail deer with a waterfowl operation. Most deer don't have webbed feet and you've probably never seen a deer painted on a duck stamp. Jerry does primarily outfit for waterfowl, being in prime territory adjacent to the North

Platte River, but for a week in November each year, a few lucky deer hunters get to hunt whitetails on his property.

First impressions are important, so I drove one of Jerry's trucks into a ditch a few hours after arriving. Having made the desired impression, I then sat down with Jerry and Karen to talk a little about their operation. They own about five hundred acres along the North Platte River that ranges from thick brush to agricultural fields. There are several springs on the property that don't freeze up when the weather turns cold. Jerry has permanent pit blinds in these areas, set up with heaters. For deer, Jerry has a box blind and three tripod stands. In bad weather, the duck blinds can also be used for deer. Accommodations are excellent with brand new housing for the hunters. Karen does some catering on the side, so it goes without saying that the meals are exceptional as well.

The first morning of the hunt found fellow hunter Floridian Ken Cypress and I ready to go as Jerry entered the building. We loaded up in the truck (I wasn't driving) and headed out in the predawn darkness. The temperature was in the high twenties, the wind was calm and the sky was overcast. We transferred to a four wheeler and headed for the tripods. Ken took the western tripod and I went to the eastern tripod located about three hundred yards from the river. The morning passed quickly as the bucks were on the move searching for does. By the time Jerry came back out to get us at ten I had seen several does and five bucks. They just weren't the caliber of bucks I was looking for.

The wind started to pick up in the afternoon as I headed for the box blind and Ken headed for a tripod on the edge of a field. By the time we got settled in it was a full blown gale, complete with sand blasting. Ken toughed it out for about a half hour, when Jerry stopped by and took him back to one of the tripods in the woods. It was blowing so hard there were whitecaps on the mud puddles. I'm not even sure I could have made a hundred yard shot, the blind was rocking so much. The evening ended with me seeing just a few skittish does.

That night during dinner I told Jerry that I'd like to sit in the stand all day the next day. I've had success in the past during the middle of the day when the rut is on, so I thought I'd give it a try. The next morning, the wind had thankfully subsided to a slight breeze and the temperature was in the low twenties. I got settled back in to the eastern tripod and listened to the morning come alive. The whistling wings of ducks flashed overhead and a rooster pheasant announced his presence by the side of the river. Then, about ten minutes before legal shooting time I heard the unmistakable sound of deer approaching from the east. Two dark blobs stepped into an opening thirty yards behind me. Through my binoculars I could see that they were a doe and a fawn. Then there was a grunt behind them. "Oh no, don't do this to me," I thought to myself as I looked at my watch again. It wasn't even close to shooting time as the new dark blob emerged on the same trail. I slowly raised my binoculars and glassed the buck. He was a nice 4x4, but thankfully not a shooter. Shortly after sunrise, a doe and a fawn wandered out in front of me. That's when the big buck mentioned at the beginning of the chapter made his appearance.

As the buck started to pursue the flatheads I braced myself on the rail of the tripod and prepared for the shot. The buck trotted around for a short while and finally stopped broadside, clearing the doe and fawn. I took the opportunity and squeezed the trigger on my Browning Stainless Stalker. As the sound of a hundred and eighty grain impact reached my ears, the buck kicked his rear legs out and dashed for cover. From the buck's reaction I was confident of a good hit and began to drop my gear out of the tripod. I stripped out of my warm clothes and headed for the brush line. I quickly found a good blood trail and started to track it into the bush. I went slowly and quietly, alert for any noise in front of me. After about fifty yards I could see an especially thick swamp ahead of me and had not found the buck yet. I decided to back out and wait a few hours until Jerry was due to come in and get Ken. I dropped a hat to mark my progress and tiptoed back to my stand.

On the way out, I had seen Ken on the ground, obviously intent on something to the west. He showed up a few minutes later and explained that he had just stalked a nice 5x5 out by the pit blind, but decided not to take him. I told him what had happened and we both went back to our respective stands. An hour and a half later Ken was back at my stand saying that someone was over there calling for their dog and asked if I wanted to see if we could find my deer. I figured enough time had passed so we headed back to the spot.

We walked in, I picked up my hat, took one more step and there he was, twenty yards in front of me. We walked over and I got a close up look at the big 4x4 buck. There was no ground shrinkage here. The buck had six inch bases, twenty-five inch main beams and huge brow tines. We figured the buck would gross in the one fifties, a fact that we later verified. After taking a few pictures, Ken and I walked out, jumped on the four wheeler and headed for the ranch house. Jerry and some friends had been moving cattle all morning and were sitting around the kitchen table when I walked in. I told Jerry that I had taken a nice 3x3 with about a fifteen inch spread. Jerry wasn't buying it and said, "Bull pucky," or something like that. At least I think a bovine of some kind was involved.

4x4 whitetails just don't get much better than this Nebraska buck.

After retrieving the buck, Jerry took Ken back to the western tripod and we set up out in the fields to see what might make an appearance. As the sun set we had seen many deer, the biggest being a two and a half year old 3x4. We picked Ken up and he said that he had seen a large buck over toward the east stand. He decided to head back there in the morning.

The next morning dawned clear and calm. I set up in the western pit blind for some photography and Ken set up in the eastern tripod. I was entertained all morning by all manner of wildlife including a nice one thirty class 4x5 that walked across the field looking for does. About mid morning, I heard a shot, but thought that it was too far away to be Ken. I knew I was mistaken when I heard the drone of the four wheeler approaching me. Jerry picked me up and we headed for Ken's stand. He had taken a nice 5x5, which was the last buck that would be taken on the property for the year.

For the forth day of the hunt, Jerry let me borrow a shotgun and we headed for the western pit blind, with Jack, his big black Labrador Retriever. The morning was clear and calm with the temperature hovering right around the freezing point. It was my first waterfowl hunting in over twenty years and the rust definitely showed as I blasted away in the general direction of the ducks flying in. I tried to explain to Jack that the borrowed shotgun was too short or too long or too something, but his dirty looks told me that he wasn't buying it. I also unsuccessfully tried to sell Jerry on the New York custom of firing two warning shots before taking the bird with the third shot.

At one point we had three ducks making a circle around the blind. As I watched, a streak of brown came in from above and behind the birds, and hit one of the ducks in an explosion of feathers. The falcon and duck dropped to the ground and I had just turned to Ken and Jerry to see if they saw the spectacle when a great horned owl beat the air overhead and spooked the falcon from the kill. Except that it wasn't a kill, as the duck took advantage of the situation and made a hasty get away to the pond behind us. That episode alone would have made the trip worth it. There aren't many people who can say they've watched a falcon slam into their prey.

Being a perfect Bluebird day, the hunting wasn't great by Jerry's standards, but by most people's standards it was very good. Even with a break in the middle of the day we ended up with a goose and one duck shy of our limit. The next day was a repeat of the last with Ken and I limiting out and getting to watch Jack make some great blind retrieves. It was a great week with memories to last a lifetime. I'll be back, and next time I'll bring my own shotgun and show Jack how to shoot.

Conclusion

So there you have it. The highlights (and a few lowlights) of about thirty years worth of hunting adventures. It's hard to believe that many years have passed. Hopefully there will be many more to follow. I hope that I've provided a bit of an escape into the great outdoors for you.

So what's next on the horizon? I'm headed up to British Columbia this fall with Dr. Peebles for elk, mountain goats and possibly moose. It's John's first hunt outside of New York, so I'm really looking forward to reliving some of our youth (probably at a slightly slower pace) and giving him bad advice during the trip. Actually I've already started out by telling him that it's flat as a pancake and all the traveling is done by Jeep. At least I'm pretty sure that's what the horses name is.

I burned all the complaints from my clients for the last few years before they could get to Randy, so I'm pretty sure the fall will also find me back in Colorado guiding for mule deer, looking for oxygen molecules and avoiding Hell's Canyon. Directly following that, I'll be headed up to Saskatchewan to hunt out of one of Jim Shockey's camps for whitetails. I start to shiver just thinking about it. It always seems like a good idea to head up to Canada in November when I'm sitting in my nice warm living room in May.

So it looks like I've got a busy fall ahead of me, with plenty of sunrises and sunsets to see and adventures to experience. Now it's time for me to ride into that burgundy orb on the horizon. Thanks for coming along on the ride.

Appendix

The initial editorial review of this book recommended an appendix with some of the gear I use or outfitters that I've hunted with. Following my normal reaction to any editorial suggestion, which is eerily reminiscent of a three year olds temper tantrum, I decided that it was probably a good idea. So here you have it. Since everyone has different opinions, likes and dislikes, perhaps think of this as a good starting point. Outfitter operations can change, please check your references carefully. If you don't see someone on the list that I mentioned in the book, then I booked through one of the agents below.

Outfitters or Outfitting Agents:

Cabelas Outdoor Adventures (Agent)
Multiple species
Multiple locations
Contact: outdooradventures@cabelas.com, www.cabelas.com

Kellogg's Outfitting Agency (Agent)
Multiple species
Multiple locations
Contact: kellhunt@frontiernet.net, 315-346-6306

Wayne Williamson
Virtually any African game
Several African countries
Contact: Williamson@gatorzw.com

Golden Gate Outfitters
Elk, mountain lion and mule deer

Colorado
Contact: www.sanmigueloutdoors.com

Silver Tip Outfitters
Fishing, rental boats and accommodations
Saskatchewan
Contact: www.silvertipoutfitting.com

Glenn's Gear:

Rifle: I've got several different brands, though none of the customs jobs. If I had to pick just one, I'd go with a Browning Stainless Stalker A-Bolt. The combination of reliability, accuracy, thumb safety, easily adjustable trigger and a clip has sold me on the Browning.

Bow: Several years ago, I was shooting one of those double cam bows that was screaming fast, but very touchy. Then I shot my first Mathews. It was smooth, quiet, forgiving and accurate. I can't imagine I'll ever own a different brand.

Scope: Again, I own several different brands, but I've settled on Leupold for the best bang for the buck.

Binoculars: Swarovski

Spotting Scope: Leupold

Ammunition: Federal Premium

Boots: There are many very good manufacturers out there. If I had to choose one for the most rugged terrain, I'd pick Meindl. The break in period is fairly lengthy, but the support that you get on the mountains is worth it.

Camouflage: There are many good patterns on the market. A quick inventory of my clothing indicates that I purchase Realtree the majority of the time.

Taxidermist: I do most of my own work, but with African animals or my sheep I leave the job to the professionals. I had some work done in Africa, but I wasn't entirely pleased with the results. Then I found Jonas Brothers Taxidermy Studio just outside of Denver, CO. They've done some outstanding work for me, and they're fast too.

www.ingramcontent.com/pod-product-compliance
Lightning Source LLC
LaVergne TN
LVHW040050171125
825778LV00030B/358